The POCKET Guid

AUSTRALIA

Original text by Anne Matthews

Updated by Marie Hall

© Automobile Association Developments Limited 2008
First published 2008

ISBN: 978-0-7495-5499-6

Published by AA Publishing, a trading name of Automobile Association Developments
Limited, whose registered office is Fanum House, Basing View, Basingstoke,
Hampshire RG21 4EA. Registered number 1878835.

Automobile Association Developments Limited retains the copyright in the original
edition © 1999 and in all subsequent editions, reprints and amendments

A CIP catalogue record for this book is available from the British Library

All rights reserved. No part of this publication may be reproduced, stored in a retrieval
system, or transmitted in any form or by any means – electronic, photocopying,
recording or otherwise – unless the written permission of the publishers has been
obtained beforehand. This book may not be sold, resold, hired out or otherwise
disposed of by way of trade in any form of binding or cover other than that in which it
is published, without the prior consent of the publisher. The contents of this publication
are believed correct at the time of printing. Nevertheless, AA Publishing accept no
responsibility for errors, omissions or changes in the details given, or for the
consequences of readers' reliance on this information. This does not affect your
statutory rights. Assessments of attractions are based upon the author's own
experience and contain subjective opinions that may not reflect the publisher's opinion
or a reader's experience. We have tried to ensure accuracy, but things do change, so
please let us know if you have any comments or corrections.

Colour separation: Keenes, Andover
Printed and bound in Italy by Printer Trento S.r.l.

Front cover images: (t) AA/M Langford; (b) AA/S Watkins
Back cover image: AA/L K Stow

A03404
Maps in this title produced from map data © New Holland Publishing (South Africa)
(Pty) Ltd. 2005. Transport map © Communicarta Ltd, UK

About this book

Symbols are used to denote the following categories:

➕ map reference

✉ address or location

☎ telephone number

🕐 opening times

✋ admission charge

🍴 restaurant or café on premises or nearby

Ⓜ nearest underground train station

🚌 nearest bus/tram route

🚃 nearest overground train station

⛴ nearest ferry stop

✈ nearest airport

❓ other practical information

ℹ tourist information office

➤ indicates the page where you will find a fuller description

This book is divided into four sections.

Planning pages 6–19
Before You Go; Getting There; Getting Around; Being There

Best places to see pages 20–41
The unmissable highlights of any visit to Australia

Exploring pages 42–127
The best places to visit in Australia, organized by area

Maps pages 131–144
All map references are to the atlas section. For example, Melbourne has the reference ➕ 137 D5 – indicating the page number and grid square in which it is to be found

Contents

Planning

Before You Go

WHEN TO GO

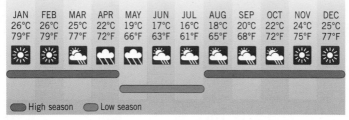

JAN	FEB	MAR	APR	MAY	JUN	JUL	AUG	SEP	OCT	NOV	DEC
26°C	26°C	25°C	22°C	19°C	17°C	16°C	18°C	20°C	22°C	24°C	25°C
79°F	79°F	77°F	72°F	66°F	63°F	61°F	65°F	68°F	72°F	75°F	77°F

High season   Low season

The temperatures listed above are the **average daily maximum** for each month in Sydney. Australia has a range of climates because of its size, geographical location and lack of high mountain ranges.

During the summer months (December to February) the southern states are the best places to visit, while Western Australia, the Northern Territory and Queensland are hot and humid.

November to April is the wet season in northern Queensland and parts of Western Australia and the Northern Territory, bringing tropical cyclones. Most of the rainfall in the Great Barrier Reef occurs in January and February.

Winter (June to August) is the best time to visit the north, west and Red Centre.

WHAT YOU NEED

		UK	Germany	USA	Netherlands	Spain
● Required	Some countries require a passport to remain valid					
○ Suggested	for a minimum period (usually at least six months)					
▲ Not required	beyond the date of entry contact their consulate or embassy or your travel agent for details.					
Passport (or National Identity Card where applicable)		●	●	●	●	●
Visa (regulations can change – check before you travel)		●	●	●	●	●
Onward or Return Ticket		▲	▲	▲	▲	▲
Health Inoculations (tetanus and polio)		▲	▲	▲	▲	▲
Health Documentation (▶ 9, Health Advice)		▲	▲	▲	▲	▲
Travel Insurance		○	○	○	○	○
Driving Licence (national) and International Driving Permit		●	●	●	●	●
Car Insurance Certificate		●	●	●	●	●
Car Registration Document		●	●	●	●	●

ADVANCE PLANNING
WEBSITES
www.australia.com
www.planbooktravel.com

TOURIST OFFICES AT HOME

In the UK
Australian Tourist Commission
✉ Gemini House
10–18 Putney Hill
London SW15 6AA
☎ 020 8780 2229

In the USA
Australian Tourist Commission
✉ 2049 Century Park East
Suite 1920
Los Angeles CA 90067
☎ 310/229 4870

HEALTH ADVICE
Insurance
British and certain other nationals
are eligible for free basic care at
public hospitals but it is strongly
recommended that all travellers
take out a comprehensive medical
insurance policy.

Dental services
Dentists are plentiful and the
standard of treatment is high –
as are the bills. In an emergency
go to the casualty wing
(emergency room) of a local
hospital, or locate a dentist from
the local telephone book. Medical
insurance is essential.

TIME DIFFERENCES

GMT	Sydney	Germany	USA (NY)	Netherlands	Spain
12 noon	10PM	1PM	7AM	1PM	1PM

Australia has three time zones.
The eastern states and ACT follow
Eastern Standard Time, which is
10 hours ahead of GMT (GMT+10).
South Australia and the Northern
Territory follow Central Standard
Time (GMT+9:30) and Western

Australia follows Western Standard
Time (GMT+8).
  Daylight Saving Time varies from
state to state and is not observed
in Western Australia, Queensland
and the Northern Territory.

WHAT'S ON WHEN

As a nation, Australia spends a considerable amount of time in holiday and party mode. There are nine annual national public holidays, and each state holds at least one major festival each year. These range from the highbrow Adelaide, Melbourne and Sydney arts festivals to sporting carnivals and the bizarre Henley-on-Todd Regatta at waterless Alice Springs.

January

Mid- to late Jan: *Australian Open* (tennis), Melbourne.
January 26: *Australia Day* holiday.
All month: *Sydney Festival* (performing arts).

February

Chinese New Year, around Australia.
End Feb: *Gay and Lesbian Mardi Gras,* Sydney.
Tropfest (short film festival), various capital cities.
Feb/Mar: *Adelaide Festival of Arts* and *Adelaide Fringe Festival* (even-numbered years only).
Perth International Arts Festival.

March

Early Mar: *Australian Formula One Grand Prix,* Melbourne.
Early to mid-Mar: *Canberra National Multicultural Festival.*

WOMADelaide (world music festival), Adelaide.
Late Mar or early Apr: *Barossa Vintage Festival* (odd-numbered years only), Barossa Valley.
Royal Easter Show, Sydney.

April

April 25: *Anzac Day* holiday.
Variable: *Melbourne International Comedy Festival.*
East Coast Roots and Blues Festival, Byron Bay.

May

Early May: *Bangtail Muster,* Alice Springs.

June

Wintersun Carnival, Gold Coast.
Variable: *Out of the Box Festival* for 3–8 year olds (even-numbered years), Brisbane.

July

Mid-Jul: *Camel Cup Carnival* (camel races), Alice Springs.
Darwin Cup Carnival (horse races).

NATIONAL HOLIDAYS

JAN	FEB	MAR	APR	MAY	JUN	JUL	AUG	SEP	OCT	NOV	DEC
2		(2)	1(3)		1						2

1 January	New Year's Day
26 January	Australia Day
March/April	Good Friday
March/April	Easter Monday
25 April	Anzac Day
Second Mon in June	Queen's Birthday
(WA: last Mon in Sep)	
25 December	Christmas Day
26 December	Boxing Day

In addition, individual states have public holidays throughout the year for agricultural shows, eg Brisbane Royal Show, Royal Canberra Show, Alice Springs and Hobart shows; regattas and race days, eg Melbourne Cup Day, Adelaide Cup Day and Hobart Regatta Day.

Late July: *Royal Darwin Show.*
Brisbane Festival (performing arts, even-numbered years).

August
Mid-Aug: *City to Surf* (fun run), Sydney.
Aug to Sep: *Festival of Darwin.*
Late Aug: *Alice Springs Rodeo.*

September
Late Sep: *AFL Grand Final* (Australian Rules football), Melbourne.
Mid-Sep to mid-Oct: *Floriade Spring Festival,* Canberra.
Henley-on-Todd Regatta, Alice Springs.
Festival Cairns (performing arts).

October
Mid-Oct: *Gold Coast Indy Carnival* (motor race).
Manly International Jazz Festival, Sydney.
Melbourne International Arts Festival.

November
First Tue: *Melbourne Cup* (horse race).
Late Nov: *Fremantle Festival.*

December
Late Dec: *Hobart Summer Festival.*

Getting There

BY AIR

All major airlines operate services to Australia. Qantas, the Australian national airline, flies from London to Australia's international airports. Flights from Europe take between 20 and 30 hours; flights from North America take about 15 hours. Many other international carriers such as British Airways, Singapore Air, Malaysia Airlines and Cathay Pacific fly to state capitals, with Melbourne and Sydney being the busiest. All have good facilities and links to their major cities.

NEW SOUTH WALES
Sydney Airport

The Sydney Airport (**www.**sydneyairport.com.au) is located 10km (6 miles) from the city centre and can be reached by taxi, bus or train.

The Sydney Airporter bus runs every 15 minutes and operates a door-to-door service from the airport to a variety of accommodation in the city, around Darling Harbour and Kings Cross.

A train service – the Airport Link (**www.**airportlink.com.au) – runs a fast service straight into Central Station every 10–15 minutes during peak times.

Melbourne Airport

Melbourne Airport (**www.**melair.com.au) is slightly further out of the city, being 25km (15 miles) away, and can be reached by taxi or shuttlebus.

Taxis are expensive but the most convenient form of transfer, whereas the Skybus Super Shuttle (**www.**skybus.com.au) is less expensive and operates a 24-hour service between Melbourne airport and Southern Cross Station downtown. Buses depart from the airport every 15 minutes between 6am and 9pm and once hourly between 1am and 5am.

There is also a free minibus shuttle service between Southern Cross Station and hotels in the Central Business District (CBD).

QUEENSLAND
Brisbane

Situated 13km (8 miles) from the city, Brisbane Airport (**www.**bne.com.au) can be reached by taxi, train and bus.

Taxis are direct but expensive and can be found outside all terminals.

Airtrain (**www.**airtrain.com.au) is a fast and effective service that runs every 15 minutes from outside the terminals at the domestic and international airports. Trains stop at Bowen Hills, Brunswick Street, Central, Roma Street, South Brisbane and Southbank and run half-hourly to the Gold Coast.

The cheapest transfer option is to take the Skytrans shuttle bus which runs to the city every 30 minutes during the hours 5.45am to 11.15pm.

The Airporter bus is a transfer service that runs every hour to the Gold Coast but is very expensive.

Cairns

Also in Queensland, Cairns Airport (**www.**cairnsairport.com.au) is 7km (5 miles) outside the town and can easily be reached by taxi. The airport shuttle bus service, Cairns Airporter Shuttle bus, operates inexpensive transfers between the airport and most hotels.

NORTHERN TERRITORY
Darwin

Some 12km (7 miles) from the city, Darwin Airport is easily reached by taxi (expensive) or the Darwin Airport Shuttle Service (inexpensive) which transfers from the airport to hotel accommodation.

SOUTH AUSTRALIA
Adelaide

Just 7km (4 miles) from the city, Adelaide Airport (**www.**aal.com.au) has good links to the city by taxi or by Skylink, a shuttle service running every half hour from 6am to 9.30pm Monday to Friday and hourly on the weekends.

WESTERN AUSTRALIA
Perth

Perth Airport (**www.**perthairport.net.au) is situated 20km (12 miles) from the city and can be reached by taxi (expensive) or the Perth Airport Shuttle bus (reasonable) which runs to Perth city as well as Fremantle, stopping at most central accommodation areas.

BY SEA

Many world cruises dock at major port cities in Australia as part of their itinerary. An informative website on sea travel is **www.**cruisecritic.com

Getting Around

PUBLIC TRANSPORT
Internal flights Australia has a wide network of domestic and regional air services. Qantas (**www.**qantas.com.au), Jetstar (**www.**jetstar.com.au) and Virgin Blue (**www.**virginblue.com. au) are the main domestic airlines, and often offer discount deals on accommodation and car rental as well as flights.

Trains Most capital cities have frequent services between business districts and the suburbs. Long-distance trains offer sleeping berths and reclining seats, and most interstate trains have dining or buffet cars. If you are booking ahead from outside Australia, enquiries and reservations are handled by Rail Australia (**www.**railaustralia.com.au).

Bus travel Excellent long-distance express bus services run daily between major cities, serviced by McCafferty's Greyhound (☎ 132 030 or 131 499). Coaches are non-smoking, have air-conditioning and bathrooms. Tasmania is serviced by Tasmanian Redline Coaches (☎ 1300 360 000) and Tassie Link (☎ 03 6257 0293).

Ferries The only regular interstate ferry services are the overnight Spirit of Tasmania passenger/vehicle ferries between Melbourne and Devonport in Tasmania (daily service; twice daily during summer) and Sydney and Devonport (twice weekly in winter, three times weekly at other times). For more information, contact ☎ 1800 634 906; **www.**spiritoftasmania.com.au

Urban transport Most state capital cities have good train services and/or frequent bus services that operate between the city centre and the suburbs. Perth, Brisbane and Sydney also have regular local ferry services. Trams or light railways run in Melbourne, Adelaide and Sydney.
For transport information in Sydney: ☎ 131500; **www.**131500.com.au
Melbourne: ☎ 131 638; **www.**metlinkmelbourne.com.au
Perth: ☎ 13 62 13;

www.transperth.wa.gov.au
Brisbane: ☎ 13 12 30;
www.translink.com.au
Adelaide: ☎ (08) 0218 2362;
www.transadelaide.com.au

Taxis Except in some country towns, all taxis in Australia display the fare on a meter. Taxis can be booked or stopped on the street.

DRIVING
Drive on the left.

Car rental Rental cars are available at major air and rail terminals and from cities throughout Australia. It is advisable to book ahead, especially during December and January. Most rental companies offer advice and provide relevant guides and maps.

If your rental car breaks down you should contact the rental company, which will arrange to send road service to your location and repair the vehicle. Alternatively, most service stations will be able to assist or, at least, direct you to the nearest repair centre.

Speed limit on motorways:
100–110kph (62–68mph)
Speed limit on urban roads:
40–60kph (52–37mph)

Obey the speed limits. There are speed cameras throughout the country and hefty speeding fines.

It is compulsory to wear seat belts at all times.

Random breath-testing. Never drive under the influence of alcohol.

Filling stations are plentiful, except in some Outback areas, but business hours may vary. Most service stations accept international credit cards.

CONCESSIONS
Students/Youths Young visitors should join the International Youth Hostels Federation before leaving their own country. Australia has a widespread network of youth and backpacker hostels. International Student or Youth Identity Cards may entitle the holder to discounts.
Senior citizens Many attractions offer a discount for senior citizens; the age limit varies from 60–65. However, few discounts on travel are available to overseas senior citizens, as an Australian pension card is usually required to qualify.

Being There

TOURIST OFFICES

● Canberra Visitor Centre (ACT)
✉ 330 Northbourne Avenue,
Dickson 2602 ☎ (02) 6205 0044
www.canberratourism.com.au

● Sydney Visitor Centre (NSW)
✉ Corner of Argyle and Playfair
streets, The Rocks ☎ (02) 9240
8788; **www.**visitnsw.com.au

● Queensland Travel Centre
✉ 30 Makerston Street, Brisbane
4000 ☎ (07) 3535 4557;
www.queenslandtravel.com

● Western Australia Visitor Centre
✉ Corner of Forrest Place and
Wellington Street, Perth 6000
☎ (08) 9483 1111;
www.visitwa.com.au

● Tourism NT
✉ Tourism House, 43 Mitchell
Street, Darwin 0800 ☎ (08) 8999
3900; **www.**tourismnt.com

● South Australia Visitor and Travel
Centre ✉ 18 King William Street,
Adelaide 3000 ☎ (08) 8303 2220;
www.southaustralia.com

● Melbourne Visitor Information
Centre ✉ Federation Square,
Melbourne 3000 ☎ (03) 9658
9658; **www.**visitvictoria.com.au

● Tasmanian Travel and Information
Centre ✉ 20 Davey Street, Hobart
7000 ☎ (03) 6230 8233
www.discovertasmania.com

EMBASSIES AND CONSULATES

UK ☎ (02) 6270 6666; Canberra
Germany ☎ (02) 6270 1911;
Canberra
USA ☎ (02) 6214 5600; Canberra
Netherlands ☎ (02) 6273 3111;
Canberra
Spain ☎ (02) 6273 3555; Canberra

TELEPHONES

Long-distance calls within Australia
(STD) and International Direct
Dialling (IDD) can be made on
public payphones. Public
payphones accept coins and
various phonecards, which are
available from retail outlets in
denominations of AU$5, AU$10 and
AU$20. The International Direct
service gives access to over 50
countries for collect or credit card
calls. Phones that accept credit
cards can be found at airports,
central city locations and hotels.
A Telstra PhoneAway prepaid card

OPENING HOURS

- ● Shops
- ● Offices
- ● Banks
- ● Post Offices
- ● Mseums/Monuments
- ● Pharmacies

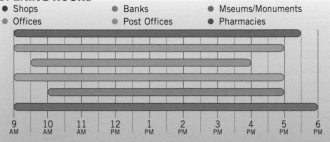

| 9 AM | 10 AM | 11 AM | 12 PM | 1 PM | 2 PM | 3 PM | 4 PM | 5 PM | 6 PM |

Shops: Hours vary from state to state. Many supermarkets and department stores stay open until 9pm on Thu and/or Fri. Some supermarkets in larger cities are open daily until midnight.

Banks: Open Mon–Fri 9–5. Some open Saturday morning.
Museums: Hours may vary.
Pharmacies: Some are open longer hours, including 24-hour services in larger cities.

enables you to use virtually any phone in Australia with all call costs charged to the card.

EMERGENCY TELEPHONE NUMBERS
Police: 000
Fire: 000
Ambulance: 000

INTERNATIONAL DIALLING CODES
To call from Australia to:
UK: 0011 44
Germany: 0011 49
USA/Canada: 0011 1
Netherlands: 0011 31
Spain: 0011 34

POSTAL SERVICES
Post offices Australia Post (**www.**auspost.com.au) offices can be found throughout the country; often combined with a general store in smaller places. Postal and poste restante services are available. Mail boxes are red with a white 'P'.

ELECTRICITY
The power supply is: 220/240 volts, 50 cycles AC.

Sockets accept three-flat-pin plugs so you may need an adaptor. If your appliances are 110v check if there is a 110/240v switch; if not you will need a voltage converter.

Universal outlets for 240v or 110v shavers are usually found in leading hotels.

CURRENCY AND FOREIGN EXCHANGE

The monetary unit of Australia is the Australian dollar (AU$) and the cent (100¢ = AU$1).

Coins come in 5¢, 10¢, 20¢, 50¢ and $1 and $2 denominations, and there are $5, $10, $20, $50 and $100 notes.

Major credit cards are accepted in all large cities and most airports and banks have facilities for changing foreign currency and traveller's cheques.

HEALTH AND SAFETY

Sun advice The sun in Australia is extremely strong, especially in summer. Wear a hat and sunglasses, and avoid sunbathing in the middle of the day. Use a high-SPF sunscreen.

Drugs Prescription and non-prescription drugs are available from pharmacies. Visitors may import up to three months' supply of prescribed medication: bring a doctor's certificate.

Safe water It is safe to drink tap water throughout Australia. Bottled mineral water is widely available.

Personal safety The usual safety precautions should be taken. Walking in the bush and swimming have their hazards.
● Hitchhiking is not recommended and is strongly discouraged by the Australian government.
● Women should avoid walking alone at night.
● If bushwalking or camping, leave an itinerary with friends. Wear boots, socks and trousers.

TIPS/GRATUITIES

Yes ✓ No ✗

Restaurants (if service not included)	✓	10%
Cafés/bars	✗	
Taxis	✗	
Porters	✓	$1–$2/bag
Chambermaids	✗	
Cloakroom attendants	✗	
Hairdressers	✗	
Theatre/cinema usherettes	✗	
Toilets	✗	

● Take care and heed warning signs when swimming, whether in the sea or fresh water (crocodiles!)
● Avoid swimming at beaches in the northern parts of Australia during the wet season (Nov–Apr), due to deadly box jellyfish.
● Surf only on patrolled beaches and stay between the flags.

PHOTOGRAPHY

What to photograph: The wilderness, Barrier Reef, mountains, natural scenery and modern architecture.

What not to photograph: Many Aboriginal people do not wish to be photographed. Always ask permission before taking photographs of Indigenous Australians or scared sites.

When to photograph: In the Outback the light can be intense; best to photograph early in the morning or late afternoon. Allow for reflected light at coastal locations.

MEDIA

What's on The entertainment scene in capital cities is covered by the major newspapers. The *Sydney Morning Herald* Metro section (in Friday's edition) is a comprehensive look at entertainment in Sydney during the next week. You can also visit **www.**citysearch.com.au for nationwide entertainment listings.

CLOTHING SIZES

Australia	UK	Europe	USA	
36	36	46	36	
38	38	48	38	
40	40	50	40	
42	42	52	42	
44	44	54	44	**Suits**
46	46	56	46	
7	7	41	8	
7.5	7.5	42	8.5	
8.5	8.5	43	9.5	
9.5	9.5	44	10.5	
10.5	10.5	45	11.5	**Shoes**
11	11	46	12	
14.5	14.5	37	14.5	
15	15	38	15	
15.5	15.5	39/40	15.5	
16	16	41	16	
16.5	16.5	42	16.5	**Shirts**
17	17	43	17	
8	8	34	6	
10	10	36	8	
12	12	38	10	
14	14	40	12	
16	16	42	14	**Dresses**
18	18	44	16	
6.5	4.5	38	6	
7	5	38	6.5	
7.5	5.5	39	7	
8	6	39	7.5	
8.5	6.5	40	8	**Shoes**
9	7	41	8.5	

Best places to see

1 Blue Mountains, New South Wales

www.bluemts.com.au

For a complete change to Sydney's waterfront glamour, visit these nearby mountains to experience the great natural beauty of their geological wonders.

This is one of Australia's most popular holiday destinations. Visitors come to the Blue Mountains to experience their wild grandeur, mist-filled valleys, rich Aboriginal and European heritage, and to escape the summer heat. The cold winters allow visitors to enjoy the charm of open fires. Just two hours by road or train from Sydney, the mountains get their name from their blue haze.

There is so much to do and see here, from just taking in the panoramic views from the many escarpment lookouts to walking in the temperate rainforests which line the ravines and valleys. Waterfalls cascade off the cliffs into valleys far below, where they join streams that disappear into dense vegetation. The golden brown of ancient, weathered rock faces, formed by the action of the elements over millions of years, contrasts with the distinctive blue-green of the mountain vegetation.

Because of the great range and diversity of land forms and plant communities, and its habitats sheltering rare or endangered fauna, the Greater Blue Mountains region became a World Heritage Site in 2000. In addition to its natural sights and adventure sports, there are myriad galleries, antiques shops, gardens, museums and fine eating establishments to enjoy. The Katoomba Scenic Railway and the Sceniscender provide unique perspectives of their surroundings while just over the range are the famous Jenolan Caves with their amazing limestone formations.

🔢 137 C7 🚉 From Sydney; stops at various mountain towns. Driving is another option 🅿 A wide range of accommodation from B&Bs to five star. Many tour companies operate day tours from Sydney 🛈 Information centres ✉ Great Western Highway, Glenbrook; ✉ Echo Point, Katoomba ☎ 1300 653 408 or 1800 641 227 🕐 Glenbrook: Mon–Fri 9–5, Sat–Sun 8.30–4.30. Closed 25 Dec

2 Cairns and District, North Queensland

www.tropicalaustralia.com.au

Cairns is the perfect base for a superb nature-based holiday allowing trips to the World Heritage-listed reefs and rainforests as well as the dry Outback.

With its international airport, well-developed tourism infrastructure and proximity to natural attractions such as the Great Barrier Reef, tropical rainforests and Atherton Tableland, Cairns is the 'tourist capital' of North Queensland. Here are dozens of hotels, restaurants and shops, and many options for cruises – as well as diving, fishing or

snorkelling trips – to the reef. Excellent beaches stretch to the north and south, and adventure activities like whitewater rafting and bungee jumping are popular. Around town you can visit the Cairns Museum and the Pier Marketplace, or just wander the streets and waterfront to soak up the city's relaxed, tropical atmosphere. North of the city is the pretty coastal town of Port Douglas, while further afield are Mossman and the Daintree rainforests.

Inland from Cairns, the cool upland region of the Atherton Tableland, with its fertile farming land, volcanic lakes, waterfalls and rainforest, presents a striking contrast to the hot, humid coast. Kuranda (27km/17 miles away) offers colourful markets, a fauna sanctuary and rainforest interpretation centre. You can reach Kuranda by road, on the spectacular Skyrail Rainforest Cableway, or by travelling on the famous Kuranda Scenic Railway, which winds its way up the Great Dividing Range.

For a complete change, take a trip inland to the Gulf Savannah country and sample the hospitality of the Outback locals. Discover the grasslands, wetlands, escarpments and the Undara Lava Tubes.

✚ 135 C5 🖐 Inexpensive–expensive ✗ Cairns
❓ Huge variety of accommodation from backpacker to five star. Car rental is relatively expensive but there are many bus services and tours to all popular destinations
🛈 Tourism Tropical North Queensland ✉ 51 The Esplanade, Cairns ☎ (07) 4051 3588 🕓 Daily; Port Douglas Tourist Information Centre ✉ 23 Macrossan Street, Port Douglas ☎ (07) 4099 5599 🕓 Daily; Kuranda Visitor Information Centre ☎ (07) 4093 311 🕓 Daily

3 Gold Coast, Queensland

www.goldcoasttourism.com.au

Although not to everyone's liking, the brash and sometimes crass Gold Coast reveals a very different side of Australia from its natural wonders.

It would be difficult not to have a good time on this lively, highly developed 70km (43-mile) strip of coastline to the south of Brisbane. Stretching down to Coolangatta on the New South Wales border, the Gold Coast offers consistently warm temperatures and an average of 300 days of sunshine each year. The sandy beaches are lapped by clear blue waters that are perfect for swimming, surfing and all kinds of water sports, and there is a smorgasbord of man-made attractions and entertainment.

The heart of the action is the appropriately named Surfers Paradise, the main town, which offers excellent shopping and dining and a host of nightlife options, including the glossy Jupiters

Casino at nearby Broadbeach. Many of the Gold Coast's attractions are particularly appealing to children, and theme parks like Dreamworld, Warner Bros Movie World, Wet 'n' Wild Water World and the excellent Sea World are extremely popular. There are many fine golf courses in the area, you can take a cruise to tranquil South Stradbroke Island, go water-skiing, or even sample the daredevil sport of bungee jumping. The Coast's list of things to do is almost endless.

If you prefer to stay somewhere quieter, the southern area around Coolangatta offers a less frenetic pace – and fewer high-rise buildings. This is also the location of Currumbin Wildlife Sanctuary. When you've had enough of the coast, a short trip to the hinterland, particularly to Lamington National Park (➤ 71) or the delightful mountain town of Mount Tamborine, is a rewarding experience. Excellent scenery and a cooler environment, with rainforest walking trails and a diversity of art and craft shops, make this town a great day trip.

➕ 137 B8 🚌 Coach transfers (from Brisbane) 🚆 Gold Coast (from Brisbane) ✈ Coolangatta
ℹ Gold Coast Tourism Bureau ✉ Cavill Avenue, Surfers Paradise ☎ (07) 5538 4419 🕐 Mon–Fri 8.30–5.30, Sat 9–5, Sun 9–3.30

4 Great Barrier Reef, Queensland

www.gbrmpa.gov.au
www.queenslandholidays.com
www.queenslandtravel.com

The Great Barrier Reef is often described as the eighth wonder of the world, and a visit to this marine wonderland will be long remembered.

Running parallel to the Queensland coast for over 2,000km (124 miles) – from Papua New Guinea to just south of the Tropic of Capricorn – the Great Barrier Reef is the world's largest living structure. This extraordinary ecosystem is, in fact, made of over 2,000 linked reefs and around 700 islands and fringing reefs, and is composed of and built by countless tiny coral polyps and algae. This famous natural attraction is protected by its Great Barrier Reef Marine Park status and World Heritage listing.

The reef itself is home to many different types of coral: some are brightly coloured, while others, like the aptly-named staghorns, take on strange formations. The reef's tropical waters host an incredible variety of marine life – everything from tiny, luminously coloured fish to sharks, manta rays, turtles and dolphins. There are many ways to view and explore this fabulous underwater world: scenic

flights, boat trips, snorkelling or scuba diving, and glass-bottom or semi-submersible boat trips are all available.

For the very best Great Barrier Reef experience, it is possible to stay right on the reef. The idyllic coral cays of Green Island, Heron Island and Lady Elliot Island offer resort accommodation, while Lady Musgrave is for campers only. Other options are to base yourself at a coastal resort (Townsville, Cairns and Port Douglas in the north, or the Whitsunday Islands further south are the best bets) or on one of the many non-reef islands. Some island suggestions are Lizard, Dunk and Magnetic Island in the north; Hayman, South Molle and Hamilton in the Whitsunday region; and Great Keppel Island in the south.

✚ 135 C6 🚌 or ✈ Proserpine, Townsville, Cairns
🛈 Queensland Travel Centre ✉ 30 Makerston Street, Brisbane ☎ (07) 3535 4557 🕐 Mon–Fri 8.30–5

5 Great Ocean Road, Victoria

www.greatoceanrd.org.au

A journey along Australia's most spectacular road reveals superb coastal scenery, charming old resorts and fishing villages, and a forested hinterland.

Extending from Torquay to Port Fairy, Victoria's Great Ocean Road snakes its way along the state's southwest coast for a distance of 300km (185 miles). Geelong, 75km (46 miles) from Melbourne, is a good starting point and nearby Bells Beach, one of Australia's surfing meccas, is a good spot to get in the mood for this oceanside drive.

The quiet village of Anglesea is famous for the kangaroos that roam its local golf course, while Lorne offers fine beaches, a delightful seaside resort atmosphere and forested hillsides inland. Beyond here are the fishing town of Apollo Bay and Otway National Park – an irresistible combination of rugged coastline and lush inland rainforest.

The coast is most dramatic as you reach Port Campbell National Park. The spectacular formations here known as the Twelve Apostles are the result of erosion caused by wind, rain and the stormy Southern Ocean. The picturesque town of Port Campbell is an ideal base for exploring.

Further west along this wild coastline, the aptly named Shipwreck Coast is famous for migrating whales which give birth here between May and August each year. The Great Ocean Road proper ends at the charming fishing village of Port Fairy, where there are over 50 National Trust-listed buildings, beaches and coastal cruises to enjoy.

➕ 137 F5 🚌 V line: Apollo Bay to Warrnambool, Fri only; driving is the best option 🚌 From Geelong to Warrnambool ❓ Great Ocean Walk: from Apollo Bay to the Twelve Apostles; www.greatoceanwalk.com.au ℹ️ Geelong and Great Ocean Road Visitor Centre ✉️ Princes Highway, Geelong ☎ 1800 620 888 or (03) 5275 5797 ⏰ Daily 9–5

6 Kakadu National Park, Northern Territory

www.deh.gov.au/parks/kakadu
www.ntholidays.com

Australia's largest national park is both a superb tropical wilderness and a treasure house of ancient Aboriginal art and culture.

Covering almost 20,000sq km (7,720sq miles) to the east of Darwin, this vast World Heritage-listed national park is one of Australia's most spectacular attractions. Much of Kakadu is a flat, river-crossed floodplain that transforms into a lake during the wet season, but this large area is backed by forested lowlands, hills, and the dramatic 250m (820ft) cliffs of the Arnhem Land escarpment. The extraordinary wildlife within this varied terrain ranges from estuarine crocodiles to dingoes, wallabies, snakes, goannas and over 280 species of birds.

There is much evidence of the area's long Aboriginal occupation, which may have endured for an incredible 50,000 years. Aboriginal-owned Kakadu includes Nourlangie and Ubirr rocks, where you can see fine examples of Aboriginal rock art, estimated to be around 20,000 years old. Among the park's scenic highlights are the spectacular Jim Jim Falls and Twin Falls that tumble off the escarpment, and Yellow Water – a tranquil waterhole and wetlands area, home to prolific birdlife.

During the wet season (November to April) many of the roads are impassable, so the best time to visit Kakadu is during the 'Dry' (May to October). Much of the park can be explored in a normal vehicle, but a four-wheel drive is necessary for off-road travelling. General information is available from Bowali Visitor Centre, but the Warradjan Aboriginal Cultural Centre at Yellow Water provides a deeper insight into the area's Indigenous culture and history. To see something of modern Aboriginal life, you can visit neighbouring Arnhem Land; this is Aboriginal land and permits are required to visit, so a tour is the only real option.

✚ 134 B2 ▧ Moderate ❙❙ Cafés in the area ($–$$)
✖ Jabiru ❓ Guided walks from visitor centre
ℹ Bowali Visitor Centre ✉ Kakadu Highway
☎ (08) 8938 1121 ◷ Daily 8–5

7 The Kimberley, Western Australia

www.kimberleytourism.com

In the far north of Western Australia, the Kimberley is one of the continent's remotest and most spectacular regions.

Explored and settled as late as the 1880s, the Kimberley is extremely rugged and very sparsely settled – the population of just 25,000 lives in Aboriginal settlements, on enormous cattle stations, and in a few small towns. This vast region of 420,000sq km (162,120sq miles) is generally divided into two main areas, the West and East Kimberley.

The tropical town of Broome, with its multicultural population, pearling history and fabulous beaches, is the ideal starting point for exploring the western region. The nearby settlement of Derby has an interesting Royal Flying

Doctor Service base, while inland attractions include the dramatic Geikie Gorge National Park, which has a 14km (9-mile) long gorge.

You can reach the East Kimberley by driving north and east from Broome or flying to Kununurra, a town near the Northern Territory border and the base for the ambitious 1960s and 1970s Ord River Irrigation Scheme. This project created the vast Argyle and Kununurra lakes – welcome breaks in the otherwise arid landscape. From here you can visit the Argyle Diamond Mine, then travel north to the remote port of Wyndham, or south to the wondrous Bungle Bungles. Contained within Purnululu National Park, 'discovered' only in 1983, and given World Heritage status in 2003, these spectacular rock formations, up to 300m (985ft) high, are composed of extremely crumbly silica and sandstone eroded into beehive-like shapes.

Other attractions worth seeing in this wild, last-frontier landscape include the Aboriginal rock art sites of Mirima National Park near Kununurra; Windjana Gorge National Park, reached via the small town of Fitzroy Crossing; and the amazing Wolfe Creek Crater – an enormous depression created by a meteorite.

➕ 133 B5 ✈ Broome or Kununurra ❓ Best visited Apr–Oct. Rental of a four-wheel drive vehicle is recommended. Purnululu National Park closed Jan–Mar ℹ West Kimberley Tourist Bureau ✉ Corner of Broome Highway and Bagot Road, Broome; East Kimberley Tourist Bureau ✉ Coolibah Drive, Kununurra; Broome Tourist Bureau ☎ (08) 9192 2222; Kununurra Tourist Bureau ☎ (08) 9168 1177 🕐 Daily, generally 9–4

8 Sydney Harbour and Sydney Opera House

www.sydneyoperahouse.com

Complemented by the ethereal, sail-like outlines of the famous Opera House, Sydney Harbour is the glittering jewel of Australia's most famous city.

From the day in January 1788 when the 11 convict-bearing ships of the First Fleet sailed into Port Jackson, Sydney's harbour has been the focus of this great city. A harbour cruise – be it on a luxury

boat or a humble Sydney ferry – is a must. From the water you will see the city, including the large areas of the Sydney Harbour National Park, from a new perspective. Ferries are also the best way to reach waterfront suburbs and the harbour's beaches. From Circular Quay you can take a trip to the beaches of Manly on the north side of the harbour, or to the southside suburb of Watsons Bay, close to the harbour's entrance. Ferries also visit some of the national park's islands, including historic Fort Denison.

On the harbour's southern shore, the curved roofs of the Sydney Opera House soar above Bennelong Point. Completed in 1973, after 14 years and many technical and political problems, this architectural masterpiece, designed by Danish architect Joern Utzon, still inspires controversy. However, there is no doubt that the structure's stone platform and dramatic white roofs, covered with over a million ceramic tiles, have made it one of the world's most distinctive buildings. Once you have inspected the exterior, attending a performance or taking a guided tour of the five performance halls is highly recommended. Above the magnificent harbour is the third ingredient of this classic Sydney scene: the Sydney Harbour Bridge (► 49), completed in 1932 and, with a tunnel running underground, still the major link between the south and north shores.

🚼 138 D2 ✉ Opera House: Bennelong Point ☎ Performance details (02) 9250 7777; tours: (02) 9250 7250; www.sydneyoperahouse.com 💷 Moderate–Expensive 🍴 Guillaume at Bennelong restaurant ($$$), cafés ($–$$) Ⓔ Circular Quay ❓ Guided tours 8.30–5. Performances include opera, ballet, classical music and theatre

9 Tasmania's World Heritage Area

www.park.tas.gov.au

Much of Tasmania is superb wilderness, and the island's relatively small size makes these untouched areas easily accessible.

Tasmania's wilderness is of such significant natural beauty that around 20 per cent – an incredible 1.38 million hectares (3.4 million acres) – of the state is under World Heritage protection. This land of rugged peaks, wild rivers, moorland and remote coastline also contains many sites of Aboriginal significance, while the wildlife includes Tasmanian devils, echidnas and the elusive platypus.

One of the most accessible regions in the World Heritage Area is the Cradle Mountain-Lake St Clair National Park, just 170km (105 miles) from the capital, Hobart. The alpine scenery here is truly spectacular – including high peaks such as Mount Ossa (1,617m/5,305ft), as well as the state's highest mountain, lakes, alpine moorlands and rainforests. There are many hiking trails here, the most famous of which is the five- to ten-day Overland Track in the heart of the Cradle Mountain-Lake St Clair National Park.

To the south, the Franklin-Gordon Wild Rivers National Park is particularly famous for its adventurous Franklin

River whitewater rafting. Even more remote and untamed wilderness is found in the Southwest National Park, the domain of forests, lakes and a long, deeply indented coastline. Experienced hikers will enjoy the challenge of this park's 85km (53-mile) South Coast Track. Much closer to Hobart and characterized by its heathlands and rugged dolerite ranges, is the Hartz Mountains National Park.

November to April are the best months to explore these areas, but the weather can be unpredictable at any time, changing in minutes from warm and sunny to rain, or even snow.

✠ 137 F5 ✋ Parks: inexpensive 🚌 From Hobart, Devonport and Launceston to some locations; driving is the best option ✖ Southwest National Park 🛈 Tasmanian Parks and Wildlife Service ✉ 134 Macquarie Street, Hobart ☎ 1300 135 513 or (03) 6233 6191 🕐 Mon–Fri 9–5

10 Uluṟu-Kata Tjuṯa National Park, Northern Territory

www.deh.gov.au/parks/uluṟu/
www.centralaustraliantourism.com

This 1,325ha (3,275-acre) World Heritage Site incorporates two of Australia's most spectacular sights – Uluṟu (Ayers Rock) and neighbouring KataTjuṯa (The Olgas).

Located at the centre of the continent, Uluṟu's vast bulk is an extraordinary and overwhelming sight. At 348m (1,142ft) high and with a base circumference of some 9km (5.5 miles), this is the world's largest monolith – a massive rock which is made even more dramatic by its setting on the monotonous plains of the Red Centre. Uluṟu was first sighted by Europeans in 1872, but this area has been sacred to the local Aṉangu people for tens of thousands of years. It is possible to climb Uluṟu, but the activity is discouraged by the Aṉangu landowners as the rock is a sacred site; under traditional law, climbing is prohibited to everyone except senior men initiated into Aṉangu culture. The climb can also be dangerous; 37 people have died attempting to ascend the monolith and many have been injured. Other options are to take a hiking tour of the base, and to view Uluṟu at sunset, when its normally dark red colour changes dramatically as the light fades.

Although, like Uluru, it is the tip of a vast underground formation, Kata Tjuta, 30km (18 miles) to the west, offers a rather different experience. The name means 'many heads' – an appropriate description of the 30 or so massive rocks which make up Kata Tjuta. The domes are sacred and are strictly off limits to visitors. Access is permitted on the established walking trails, but most of these should be undertaken only if you are well prepared.

A visit to the Uluru-Kata Tjuta Cultural Centre, just 1km (0.5 miles) from Uluru, is a must. This excellent complex includes displays on Aboriginal culture and history, demonstrations of traditional art and dance, and a shop that sells local arts and crafts. The base for exploring the national park is the well-designed Ayers Rock Resort village.

✛ 134 E1 ✋ Expensive 🕓 Dec–Feb daily 5–9; Mar 5.30–8.30; Apr 6–8; May 6–7.30; Jun–Jul 6.30–7.30; Aug 6–7.30; Sep 5.30–7:30; Oct 5–8; Nov 5–8.30 (parts of the park may be temporarily closed) ✖ Connellan airport ℹ Cultural centre ☎ (08) 8956 1128 🕓 Daily 7–6

Exploring

Australia is a young nation in an ancient land. Its people are from diverse backgrounds; some have been here for more than 60,000 years, but many – a third of the popuation – have arrived in only the last 60. Although proud of its pioneering history and Outback traditions, this is the world's most urbanised society, with 88 per cent of people living in towns and cities.

The Australian landscape varies greatly, encompassing lush tropical rainforests, an arid desert interior, snowy peaks and sandy beaches; but wherever you go, the scenery is spectacular, the atmosphere is laid back and the sun is likely to be shining.

New South Wales and the Australian Capital Territory

New South Wales, named by Cook in 1770 because it reminded him of south Wales, is Australia's fourth-largest state but has the largest population – almost 6.7 million. Geographically, it is made up of a series of parallel strips: a narrow coastal plain which supports the bulk of the population, the uplands of the Great Dividing Range, slopes and plains which form the state's agricultural heartland and, finally, the Outback. The climate varies from subtropical in the north to the winter snows of the mountains in the far south.

Although within the boundaries of New South Wales, the Australian Capital Territory, or ACT, is governed and administered separately. The territory and the national capital, Canberra, were created early in the 20th century to resolve the long-running rivalry between Sydney and Melbourne over which city should be the nation's capital.

www.visitnsw.com.au

45

Sydney

The nation's birthplace has developed from its humble convict beginnings into a vibrant metropolis that holds its own on the world stage. With a multicultural population of over 4 million, Sydney is the continent's largest and, many would say, most brash, city. Although the pace of life is faster here than anywhere else in Australia, Sydneysiders still know how to relax – the city's harbour, long golden beaches and surrounding bushland make sure of that.

In recent years Sydney has truly come of age as a major city and an enviable tourist destination. It has been voted 'the world's best city' by discerning travellers the world over, but perhaps the biggest accolade of all came when Sydney was chosen as the host city for the 2000 Summer Olympic Games. In addition to the fascinating convict history, museums, galleries and, of course, the 'Great Outdoors', the city offers wonderful shopping, an innovative and highly acclaimed restaurant scene and a wide choice of nightlife.

Although visitors spend most of their time in the inner city and eastern suburbs, an entirely different world lies beyond. To the north lie the glorious Northern Beaches with surf, sand and a far more relaxed lifestyle, the charming waterway of Pittwater, and the bushland of Ku-ring-gai Chase National Park. To the west, you can visit historic Parramatta and Sydney Olympic Park, the Olympic Games site. Sydney's inner suburbs also have a great deal to offer. A visit to famous Bondi, Manly or one of the many other beaches is a must.

www.seesydney.com.au

✚ 137 C7

AUSTRALIAN MUSEUM

A world-class natural history museum, this is an excellent place to learn about pre-European Aboriginal life and Australia's native fauna.

Also featured are human evolution, minerals, dinosaurs, biodiversity and a fascinating skeletons room.

www.austmus.gov.au

✚ 139 D6 ✉ 6 College Street ☎ (02) 9320 6000 🕐 Daily 9.30–5. Closed 25 Dec ✋ Moderate

DARLING HARBOUR

With its harbourside shopping and eating complexes, the delightful Chinese Garden, the Imax Theatre and National Maritime Museum, Darling Harbour is one of Sydney's most popular recreation areas. One of the best attractions here is the **Sydney Aquarium,** where you will encounter sharks, crocodiles and colourful Great Barrier Reef fish at close quarters. The nearby

futuristic building of the Australian National Maritime Museum contains several galleries covering maritime themes as diverse as the discovery of Australia and surfboard technology. Many of the exhibits are interactive. Moored outside are various vessels, including a World War II destroyer and a submarine.

www.darlingharbour.com

✚ 139 B6 ✉ Darling Harbour

☎ (02) 9240 8500 🕐 Daily 9.30–5.30

Sydney Aquarium

☎ (02) 8751 7800 🕐 Daily 9am–10pm (last admission at 9) ✋ Expensive

🚋 Monorail Darling Park

POWERHOUSE MUSEUM

Sydney's largest museum is an entertaining technological and cultural wonderland with everything from a huge 18th-century steam engine and a 1930s art deco cinema to holograms and irresistible hands-on computer displays.

www.phm.gov.au

✠ 139 B7 ✉ 500 Harris Street, Ultimo ☎ (02) 9217 0111 🕐 Daily 10–5. Closed 25 Dec ✋ Moderate

THE ROCKS

With its intriguing past and prime harbourside location, this is Sydney's tourist mecca. It was the site of Australia's first 'village' and has had a colourful history. In addition to wandering the narrow streets, sitting on the waterfront and browsing in the many shops, Rocks highlights are a lively weekend market and several small museums – including the Sydney Observatory at nearby Millers Point. Full details of the area are available from the Information Centre.

www.sydneyvisitorcentre.com

✚ 138 C2 ⓠ Circular Quay
ℹ Sydney Visitor Centre ✉ Corner of Argyle and
Playfair streets, The Rocks ☎ (02) 9240 8788
🕐 Daily 9.30–5.30. Closed 25 Dec, Good Fri

SYDNEY HARBOUR
See pages 36–37.

SYDNEY HARBOUR BRIDGE
Completed in 1932, this famous bridge is still
the primary link between the harbour's north
and south shores, although the Sydney Harbour
Tunnel now handles a large share of the traffic.
You can inspect the bridge from close up by
taking the walkway from the Rocks, and then
climbing the 200 steps of the Pylon. For really
spectacular views of the harbour and city, take
the BridgeClimb tour.

✚ 138 C1 ☎ Pylon Lookout: (02) 9247 3408;
BridgeClimb: (02) 8274 7777; www.bridgeclimb.com
🕐 Lookout and Museum: daily 10–5. Closed 25 Dec
🎟 Lookout: inexpensive; BridgeClimb: expensive
ⓠ Circular Quay

SYDNEY OPERA HOUSE
See pages 36–37.

SYDNEY TOWER
The best view in town is from the top of this 304.8m (1,000ft) tower. From the observation level there are superb 360-degree views of the city and its surroundings. The tower has two revolving restaurants; particularly spectacular at night. The more adventurous might like to try the Skywalk, which involves being harnessed to the edge of a moving, glass-floored platform outside the tower for 90 minutes.

✚ 139 C5 ✉ 100 Market Street ☎ (02) 9333 9222; www.skywalk.com.au
🕐 Tower: Sun–Fri 9–10.30, Sat 9 –11.30.
Skywalk: daily 9–10 (last skywalk 8.15pm)

TARONGA ZOO
Reached by a scenic ferry ride, Taronga is visited as much for its harbourside location as for the opportunity to meet native Australian wildlife. There are koalas, kangaroos, echidnas, wombats and Tasmanian devils here, as well as native birds and reptiles, and a large collection of other zoo animals.
www.zoo.nsw.gov.au

✚ 138 C1 (off map) ✉ Bradleys Head Road, Mosman ☎ (02) 9969 2777
🕐 Daily 9–5 ✋ Expensive 🍴 Cafés ($$) and kiosk ($) 🚌 247 ⛴ From Circular Quay

Canberra and the Australian Capital Territory (ACT)

Created out of New South Wales farmland after its site was designated in 1908, Canberra is a planned city unlike anywhere else in the nation. Designed by American architect Walter Burley Griffin, and surrounded by parks and gardens, the national capital is a pleasant environment. Canberra is the home of Australia's Federal government; 40 per cent of the 321,000 population is employed in this field. The city is full of diplomatic missions and government departments, and – appealing for the visitor – national museums and galleries. The central focus is man-made Lake Burley Griffin, a location for cruises, from where roads radiate to suburbs and wild bushland. Beyond the city, the surrounding Australian Capital Territory offers rugged Namadgi National Park, Tidbinbilla Nature Reserve and 1859 Lanyon Homestead.

www.canberratourism.com.au ✚ 137 D6

AUSTRALIAN NATIONAL BOTANIC GARDENS

Containing the world's best collection of unique Australian flora, these gardens feature more than 600 species of eucalyptus trees, a rock garden, the delightful rainforest gully, and a Tasmanian alpine garden. Self-guided arrow trails make it easy to find your way around.

Looming behind the gardens is Black Mountain (779m/2,555ft), capped by the futuristic Telstra Tower. There is a spectacular view of the city and surrounds from the tower's viewing gallery.
www.anbg.gov.au

✉ Clunies Ross Street, Acton ☎ (02) 6250 9540 🕐 Feb–Dec daily 8.30–5; Jan Mon–Fri 8.30–6, Sat–Sun 8.30–8. Closed 25 Dec ✋ Free 🍴 Café ($–$$) 🚌 34 to University then 10-minute walk ❓ Free tours

AUSTRALIAN WAR MEMORIAL

In a dramatic location at the head of Anzac Parade, this impressive monument and museum commemorates the Australians who served in various wars. Its many thousands of displays include aeroplanes, tanks, guns, military memorabilia and artworks.
www.awm.gov.au

✉ Treloar Crescent, Campbell ☎ (02) 6243 4211 🕐 Daily 10–5 ✋ Free 🍴 Cafés ($–$$) 🚌 33

NATIONAL GALLERY OF AUSTRALIA

This is the nation's premier gallery, and the ideal place to view good examples of Aboriginal and Australian art. European, Asian and American artworks are also featured, and the gallery hosts excellent travelling exhibitions.

www.nga.gov.au

✉ Parkes Place, Parkes ☎ (02) 6240 6502 ⏰ Daily 10–5. Closed Good Fri, 25 Dec ♿ Free

NATIONAL MUSEUM OF AUSTRALIA

Opened in 2001, this modern museum explores the key issues, events and people that have shaped Australia. The themed galleries employ state-of-the-art technology and feature the symbols of the nation, indigenous peoples, and stories of ordinary and famous Australians.

www.nma.gov.au

✉ Lawson Crescent, Acton Peninsula ☎ (02) 6208 5000 ⏰ Daily 9–5 ♿ Free general entry 🚌 34

PARLIAMENT HOUSE

Canberra's architectural and political centrepiece was completed in 1988, at a staggering cost of over $1,000 million. It contains the House of Representatives and the Senate, and features fine artworks and craftsmanship. Guided tours are available, and the view from the roof is superb. Also in this Parliamentary Triangle area stands the more modest 1927 Old Parliament House, now housing the National Portrait Gallery.

www.aph.gov.au

✉ Capital Hill ☎ (02) 6277 7111 ⏰ Daily 9–5 (later when Parliament is sitting). Closed 25 Dec

♿ Free 🍽 Café ($–$$) 🚌 31, 34, 39
❓ Guided tours every 20 mins. Book for
Question Time (☎ (02) 6277 4889)

QUESTACON

Also known as The National
Science and Technology Centre,
this exciting, modern complex
brings the world of science alive.
Education and entertainment are
combined brilliantly in the 170 or
so interactive exhibits.
www.questacon.edu.au
✉ King Edward Terrace, Parkes ☎ (02)
6270 2800 🕐 Daily 9–5 ♿ Moderate

What to See in New South Wales

BLUE MOUNTAINS
See pages 22–23.

BROKEN HILL
Broken Hill's harsh landscape is far removed from the waterside ambience of Sydney. This silver-mining town in far western NSW is a good Outback destination. Here you can tour one of the mines, visit the Royal Flying Doctor Service base, and take a trip to nearby Kinchega National Park or the ghost town of Silverton.
www.visitbrokenhill.com.au

🚩 136 C4 🚆 or ✈ From Sydney 🛈 Broken Hill Visitor Centre ✉ Blende Street ☎ (08) 8087 6077 🕧 Daily 8.30–5

BYRON BAY
With a wonderful climate, sandy beaches and pounding surf, 'Byron' attracts surfers, scuba divers and holidaymakers in droves. Walk to Cape Byron (Australia's most easterly point), enjoy fine restaurants, or just browse the art and craft shops. Take a drive to the hinterland rainforests or the nearby town of Mullumbimby.
www.visitbyronbay.com

🚩 137 B8 ✈ Ballina or Lismore, then a drive 🛈 Byron Bay Visitor Centre ✉ 80 Jonson Street ☎ (02) 6680 8558 🕧 Daily 9–5

COFFS HARBOUR
Tourism and banana growing are the main industries of this coastal city, which offers excellent beaches and a sunny climate. Kids will enjoy the Pet Porpoise Pool and Big Banana leisure park, while a drive inland to the picturesque town of Bellingen and rainforests of World Heritage-listed Dorrigo National Park is recommended.
www.visitcoffsharbour.com

🚩 137 B7 🚆 or ✈ From Sydney 🛈 Coffs Coast Visitor Centre ✉ Corner Pacific Highway and Maclean streets ☎ (02) 6652 1522 🕧 Daily 9–5

HUNTER VALLEY

Wine and wineries are the main attraction of
this large river valley northwest of Sydney,
centred around the town of Cessnock and the village of Pokolbin.
Grapes have been cultivated here since the 1830s and there are
now over 100 wineries in the region; many of these can be toured
and you can, of course, sample the fine wines that originate from
the area. The Hunter also has a reputation for excellent
accommodation and dining, making it a very popular weekend
destination for Sydneysiders.

www.winecountry.com.au

✚ 137 C7 🚉 Maitland, then a bus to Cessnock

ℹ Hunter Valley Wine Country Visitor Centre ✉ 455 Wine Country Drive,
Pokolbin ☎ (02) 4990 0900 🕐 Mon–Fri 9–5, Sat 9.30–5, Sun 9.30–3.30

KIAMA

One of the closest South Coast resorts to Sydney, the small town
of Kiama (90 minutes' drive away) has long enjoyed great

popularity. As well as good beaches and surfing, the town has a famous blowhole, discovered by whaler George Bass in 1797 on a voyage of coastal exploration, and many historic buildings.

Kiama is close to the charmingly rural Kangaroo Valley, and the Minnamurra Rainforest Centre within the Budderoo National Park.

www.kiama.com.au

✚ 137 D7 🚆 From Sydney

ℹ️ Kiama Visitor Centre ✉️ Blowhole Point Road ☎ (02) 4232 3322

🕐 Daily 9–5. Closed 25 Dec

LORD HOWE ISLAND

A true South Sea paradise. Dominated by sheer peaks, this World Heritage-listed small island is just 11km (7 miles) long and 2.8km (1.7 miles) at its widest. The high peaks and lower, scattered hills were created by volcanic activity, and below these lie kentia palm forests, idyllic sandy beaches, a fringing coral reef, and the clear blue waters of the island's lagoon, home to over 500 fish species.

www.lordhoweisland.info

✚ 137 C8 (off map) ✈️ From Sydney and Brisbane

ℹ️ Island Visitor Centre ☎ 1800 240 937 or (02) 6563 2114 🕐 Mon–Fri 9–4, Sun 9–12.30 ❓ Various grades of accommodation available

MYALL LAKES NATIONAL PARK

This North Coast national park encompasses both a chain of large freshwater lakes and an idyllic 40km (25-mile) coastline. You can rent a houseboat or canoe to explore the lakes, or camp and enjoy surfing and swimming off the golden beaches. The area is particularly appealing to birdwatchers and bushwalkers.
www.nationalparks.nsw.gov.au

✚ 137 C7 ☎ (02) 4984 8200 or (02) 6591 0300 ⊛ Daily ✋ Inexpensive
❓ No public transport into the park

SNOWY MOUNTAINS

In the state's far south, reached via the town of Jindabyne, this upland region encompasses **Kosciuszko National Park,** where you can ski in winter from the resorts of Thredbo and Perisher Blue. The wilderness park contains heathland and alpine vegetation, as well as Mount Kosciuszko, Australia's highest point (just 2,228m/7,310ft). In summer the area is great for bushwalking, trout fishing, horse riding and mountain biking.
✚ 137 D6

Kosciuszko National Park
✉ Snowy Region Visitor Centre, Kosciuszko Road, Jindabyne ☎ (02) 6450 5600 🕐 Winter daily 8–5.30; summer daily 8.30–5 🚌 Jindabyne and Thredbo. Perisher Blue (ski season)

SOUTHERN HIGHLANDS
Just 100km (62 miles) from Sydney, this upland region offers a blend of rugged Australian bush, rolling English-type farmland and genteel townships.

Colonial history is well represented: the charming village of Berrima dates from the early 1830s and is full of historic buildings. You can shop for crafts and antiques in Berrima, Moss Vale and Bowral, and go bushwalking in the Morton National Park.

www.southern-highlands.com.au

✚ 137 D7 🚉 Mittagong, Bowral, Moss Vale, Exeter, Bundanoon

ℹ Information Centre ✉ 62–70 Main Street, Mittagong ☎ 1300 657 559 or (02) 4871 2888 🕐 Daily 8–5.30

Queensland

Occupying an enormous chunk of the continent's northeast, Queensland is the second largest state after Western Australia. From the subtropical capital of Brisbane in the south, this vast tract of land – much of which has a hot, sunny and virtually winterless climate – stretches north to well within the tropics.

Many people come here solely to experience the Great Barrier Reef World Heritage Site, a magnificent natural wonder that lies parallel to the coast's sandy beaches and idyllic islands. But Queensland offers much more. Behind the coastal strip and the hills of the Great Dividing Range, stretches the inhospitable Outback, while in the far north are lush tropical rainforests and the Cape York Peninsula, which ends just south of Papua New Guinea.
www.queenslandholidays.com.au

Brisbane

From its crude beginnings as a penal colony – founded in 1824 as an outpost of New South Wales – and its long-standing reputation as a conservative 'country town', Brisbane has undergone a remarkable metamorphosis in recent years and has embraced progress with much enthusiasm. With a subtropical climate and relatively small population of over 1.6 million, the city has a slower pace of life than that of southern cities, and Queensland's capital has blossomed into a most attractive metropolis.

Although most visitors do not linger for long in Brisbane before heading south to the Gold Coast or north to the attractions of the coast and Great Barrier Reef, there is plenty to see and do here. The city's riverside location is an important ingredient in its charm: Brisbane stands on a sweeping bend of the Brisbane River, and a leisurely cruise or ferry ride along the river is a highlight of any trip.

There *are* museums, galleries and a few graceful old buildings here, but sunny Brisbane is a largely modern city, concerned for the most part with relaxing and enjoying the good things in life. The brilliantly designed South Bank parklands, which include a swimming lagoon and sandy beach, and the city's many parks and gardens, are ideal places to indulge in such pursuits, as are the islands and beaches of nearby Moreton Bay. You can also explore the pleasant city centre – particularly the shops and outdoor cafés of Queen Street Mall; the Riverside Centre and its ferry wharves, just off Eagle Street; and the Roma Street Parkland.

www.ourbrisbane.com

✚ 135 F7

CITY BOTANIC GARDENS

Brisbane's premier gardens are in a delightful riverside setting and provide the ideal spot for a break from sightseeing and the heat. The gardens are open around the clock. Wander among the palm trees, Bunya pines and rainforest area, or take a guided walk.

✉ Alice Street ☎ (07) 3403 0666 🍴 City Gardens Café ($–$$) ♿ Free
🚌 The Loop

MOUNT COOT-THA

It's worth making the trip to this peak, 6.5km (4 miles) from the city centre, especially at night, for the wonderful view of Brisbane and its surroundings.

You can visit the **Brisbane Botanic Gardens,** with their tropical and native flora, hiking paths and Aboriginal trails, as well as the Cosmic Skydome and Planetarium, where a dramatic image of the night sky is projected onto a dome.
www.brisbanelookout.com

Brisbane Botanic Gardens
✉ Mount Coot-tha Road, Toowong
☎ (07) 3403 2535 🕓 Sep–Mar daily
8–5.30; Apr–Aug 8–5 💲 Gardens: free;
Skydome: moderate 🍴 Café ($); restaurant
($$) 🚌 471

QUEENSLAND CULTURAL CENTRE

This modern South Bank complex includes two important museums –

the Queensland Art Gallery, with its fine collection of Australian, Aboriginal, Asian, Pacific and European art; and the Queensland Museum with some particularly good Aboriginal and natural history displays.

Nearby to the south, the large riverside South Bank Parklands is one of Australia's best urban parks, with bars, pubs, restaurants and cafés, shopping, an IMAX theatre and weekend markets. The **Queensland Maritime Museum** is also worth a visit.

www.south-bank.net.au

✉ Corner of Melbourne and Grey streets, South Brisbane ☎ Art Gallery: (07) 3840 7303; www.qag.qld.go.au. Museum: (07) 3840 7555; www.qm.qld.gov.au
🕐 Art Gallery: Mon–Fri 10–5, Sat–Sun 9–5. Museum 9.30–5 ✋ Free

Queensland Maritime Museum

✉ Stanley Street ☎ (07) 3844 5361 🕐 Daily 9.30–4.30

QUEENSLAND SCIENCENTRE

With over 170 hands-on exhibits, this is the state's largest science and technology centre. Even the most non-scientific mind, young or old, will be captivated and special shows and demonstrations are held daily.

✉ Queensland Museum, corner of Melbourne and Grey streets, South Brisbane ☎ (07) 3840 7555 🕐 Daily 9–5 ✋ Moderate

What to See in Queensland

CARNARVON GORGE NATIONAL PARK

Although it is very remote (over 250km/155 miles from the nearest town, Roma), a visit to this spectacular park is well rewarded. The Carnarvon Creek has cut through soft sandstone to create 200m (655ft) cliffs and a 30km (18-mile) long gorge. There is some good bushwalking, as well as lush vegetation and ancient Aboriginal paintings. Roads may be impassable between January and April. **www**.epa.qld.gov.au

✚ 135 E6 ✉ Carnarvon National Park, via Rolleston ☎ (07) 4984 4505
🕐 Daily ✋ Free ✖ Roma, then a drive

CAIRNS AND DISTRICT
See pages 24–25.

CHARTERS TOWERS
Once the second largest city in Queensland, with its own stock exchange, this historic town, situated 135km (84 miles) west of Townsville, was built on gold over a century ago. Today it is a living museum of grand hotels, banks and other National Trust-classified buildings. The World Theatre, built in 1891 as an international bank, now serves as a focus for arts and entertainment with a fully restored auditorium, cinema, archival centre and art gallery.

The town has a number of significant events each year, including the Australia Day (26 January) Cricket Festival, the Rodeo (Easter) at nearby Mingela and one of Australia's largest country music festivals on the May Day weekend. (See also Townsville ➤ 74.)

www.charterstowers.qld.gov.au

✚ 135 D6 🚉 or ✈ Townsville

ℹ️ Visitor Information Centre ✉ 74 Mosman Street ☎ (07) 4752 0314

🕐 Daily 9–5. Closed Good Fri, 25–26 Dec, 1 Jan

FRASER ISLAND

At 121km (75 miles) long, this extraordinary World Heritage Site is the world's largest sand island. Yet with extensive rainforest, over 40 freshwater lakes, long sandy beaches, and strangely coloured sand cliffs this is a surprisingly varied environment. The wildlife – including dingoes and wallabies – is prolific, making the island the perfect destination for nature lovers and birdwatchers. Fraser Island is reached by vehicular ferry and a four-wheel-drive vehicle is necessary, unless taking one of the many tours.

www.queenslandholidays.com.au

✚ 135 E7 ✋ Free 🚢 From Hervey Bay ℹ Hervey Bay Tourism ✉ Corner of Urraween and Maryborough Hervey roads, Hervey Bay ☎ 1800 811 728 or (07) 4125 9855 ⏰ Daily 9–5. Closed Good Friday and 25 Dec

GOLD COAST
See pages 26–27.

GREAT BARRIER REEF
See pages 28–29.

LAMINGTON NATIONAL PARK

Temperate and subtropical rainforests, wild mountain scenery with waterfalls, gorges, rock pools, caves and abundant wildlife all combine to make this World Heritage-listed national park a must-see destination for nature lovers. There are 160km (100 miles) of hiking paths to explore, as well as plenty of easy trails and a rainforest canopy trail. The most accessible and popular sections of the national park are Green Mountains and Binna Burra.
www.epa.qld.gov.au

✚ 135 F7 ✋ Free ✕ Gold Coast or Brisbane, then a drive
ℹ Green Mountains ☎ (07) 5544 0634; Binna Burra ☎ (07) 5533 3584

LONGREACH

Longreach in Queensland's Outback was the first home of the national airline Qantas (Queensland and Northern Territory Aerial Services) during the 1920s, and the town has many charming old buildings. The major attraction is the excellent **Australian Stockman's Hall of Fame** and Outback Heritage Centre – a modern complex that pays tribute to the early explorers, pioneers and settlers.

✚ 135 E5

Australian Stockman's Hall of Fame

✉ Landsborough Highway, Longreach ☎ (07) 4658 2166 🕙 Daily 9–5. Closed 25 Dec
♿ Expensive 🍴 Snack bar ($) ✖ Longreach

SUNSHINE COAST

Stretching for 65km (40 miles) to the north of Brisbane, the Sunshine Coast region has beautiful white beaches, low-key resorts, and some outstanding national parks. The stylish main resort town of **Noosa Heads** offers sandy beaches and cosmopolitan dining, while nearby attractions include cruising the Noosa River, and exploring the dunes and coloured sand cliffs of Cooloola National Park. Inland, you can tour the Blackall Range region, where there are green hills, charming villages and rich farming country.

www.sunshinecoast.org

✚ 135 E7 🚉 Nambour, then a bus
✈ Maroochydore
ℹ Tourist Information ✉ Hastings Street, Noosa Heads ☎ (07) 5447 4988 🕐 Daily 9–5. Closed 25 Dec

TOWNSVILLE

With a population of about 125,000, this historic harbourside settlement is Australia's largest tropical city. The main points of interest are the excellent Reef HQ aquarium complex, the Museum of Tropical Queensland housing relics from the wreck HMS *Pandora*, and the wildlife-rich Billabong Sanctuary. You can visit nearby Magnetic Island, with its fine beaches and abundant wildlife, and take trips to the Great Barrier Reef.

www.townsvilleonline.com.au

🗺 135 D6 🚆 or ✈ Townsville

ℹ Visitor Centre ✉ Flinders Mall ☎ (07) 4721 3660

🕐 Mon–Fri 9–5, Sat–Sun 9–1

WHITSUNDAY ISLANDS

Reached via Proserpine and the villages of Airlie Beach and Shute Harbour, these central coast islands form a very popular holiday destination. There are over 70 islands, mostly hilly and forested, with exquisite beaches and incredibly clear turquoise waters. There is a good choice of resorts – from high-class Hayman to the less sophisticated national park Long Island resort. There are plenty of day trips to the reef, and the region is perfect for sailing, snorkelling and water sports.
www.whitsundaytourism.com

➕ 135 D6 ✖ Proserpine

ℹ Whitsunday Information Centre ✉ Bruce Highway, Proserpine ⏰ Mon–Fri 9–5, Sat–Sun 9–3 ☎ (07) 4945 3711

Victoria and Tasmania

Australia's most southerly states hold many surprises – a cooler climate (including winter snows) than many would expect, tranquil farmland, rugged peaks, and coastlines lashed by the wild waters of Bass Strait, which divides Victoria from Tasmania.

Victoria, separated from New South Wales by the country's longest river, the Murray, is small and densely populated by Australian standards. From the gracious capital, Melbourne, it is easy to reach attractions that vary from dramatic coastlines to the ski fields and peaks of the Great Dividing Range.

The compact island state of Tasmania is packed with interest. Its violent convict past intrigues history lovers, while the superb coastal, mountain and wilderness scenery provides endless opportunities for outdoor activities. You can fly to Hobart and Launceston from the mainland, or take the *Spirit of Tasmania* ferry from Melbourne or Sydney to Devonport.

www.visitvictoria.com
www.discovertasmania.com.au

Melbourne

Australia's second largest city, with a population of around 3.5 million, Melbourne is very different to its glossy northern sister. Founded long after Sydney, in 1835, this more elegant, European-style city retains many grand buildings and while its citizens are regarded as more conservative than Sydneysiders, this is not borne out in any tangible way. The climate is often 'four seasons in a day' and can be very hot in summer. Melbourne's cooler winter temperatures are often accompanied by romantic, grey days.

Melbourne has much to recommend it to visitors: there are over 4,000 restaurants and the dining scene is superb; the shopping rivals that of Sydney; sport is practically a religion; and there is plenty of nightlife – including high-quality theatrical and cultural events at the Victorian Arts Centre and other venues.

A vibrant and dynamic city, bisected by the Yarra River (on which you can take a scenic cruise), the central city area contains many museums and galleries, gracious avenues such as Collins and Spring Streets, and an abundance of green open spaces. Another Melbourne delight is riding the extensive tram network; trams have practically disappeared from all other Australian cities, but in Melbourne this is very much the way to get around.

This is a city of many ethnic groups, as a visit to Chinatown and the Museum of Chinese Australian History, or the suburbs of Italian-influenced Carlton and multicultural Richmond reveal. Other enclaves are St Kilda (➤ 82–83) and South Yarra, with boutiques and the grand 1840s house, Como.

www.visitmelbourne.com

✚ 137 D5

MELBOURNE CRICKET GROUND

Visiting this most hallowed of Australia's sporting venues is a must. The city's famous cricket ground, known as the MCG, was the site of the first Australia-England test match in 1877 and the main stadium for the 1956 Olympic Games. Today, the 100,000-capacity ground is used for both cricket and Australian Rules

Football, and contains the excellent Olympic and Australian Cricket Hall of Fame.

www.mcg.org.au

✉ Yarra Park, Jolimont ☎ (03) 9657 8864 🕓 Daily 9.30–4.30. Closed Good Fri, 25 Dec ♿ Moderate 🍴 Coffee shop ($) 🚊 Trams 48, 75 ❓ Regular guided tours 10–3 on non-event days

MELBOURNE MUSEUM

This modern complex is the largest museum in the southern hemisphere. Highlights include the Science and Life Gallery, the Bunjilaka Aboriginal Centre, a 'living forest'  complete with wildlife, and an IMAX theatre.

www.melbourne.museum.vic.gov.au

✉ Carlton Gardens, Rathdowne Street ☎ 13 1102 ♿ Moderate 🚊 Trams 86, 96, City Circle

MELBOURNE OBSERVATION DECK

The view from this observation deck, on Level 55 of the tallest building in Melbourne, is simply awe-inspiring. The panorama takes in the city and Port Phillip Bay and stretches as far away as the Dandenong Ranges, about 40km (25 miles) from Melbourne.

www.melbournedeck.com.au

✉ 525 Collins Street ☎ (03) 9629 8222 🕐 Daily 10–9 👋 Moderate
🍴 Licensed café ($$) 🚋 City Circle tram

NATIONAL GALLERY OF VICTORIA

Victoria's premier art gallery displays some of the finest artwork in Australia. The international collection, featuring European Old Masters, photography and Asian, pre-Columbian and contemporary art, is housed at the revamped **NGV International**

on St Kilda Road. The Ian Potter Centre: NGV Australia, at Federation Square, contains Australian art, including Aboriginal, Colonial and contemporary works.
www.ngv.vic.gov.au

NGV International
✉ 180 St Kilda Road ☎ (03) 8620 2222 🕐 Daily 10–5. Closed Good Fri, 25 Dec 💶 Free general admission 🚊 City Circle tram, 6, 8, 72

OLD MELBOURNE GAOL

Although rather grim, this mid-19th century building is fascinating. The gaol, scene of 135 hangings – including that of the notorious bushranger Ned Kelly on 11 November 1880 – provides an idea of what colonial 19th-century prison life was like, and contains many intriguing exhibits, including death masks and a flogging triangle. ✉ Russell Street ☎ (03) 9663 7228 🕐 Daily 9.30–5. Closed Good Fri, 25 Dec and Anzac Day am ✋ Moderate 🚌 City Circle tram ❓ Atmospheric evening tours available

ST KILDA

Melbourne has many lively suburbs which provide a venue for Melburnians to let their hair down. Located on the shores of Port

Phillip Bay, St Kilda has been the city's seaside resort since the 1880s, when the pier was constructed. Its waterfront pathway is popular with walkers, cyclists and in-line skaters, and the Luna Park funfair, built in 1912, continues to be a great attraction. There are dozens of bustling cafés and restaurants, particularly on Acland Street. The Sunday arts and crafts markets are good, and you can take a cruise on the bay from the St Kilda Pier.

www.visitvictoria.com

🚋 Any St Kilda tram

ℹ️ Melbourne Visitor Information Centre ✉️ Federation Square ☎ (03) 9658 9658 🕐 Daily 9–6

What to See in Victoria

BALLARAT

Gold was discovered near Ballarat in 1851, an event that was to

bring incredible wealth to the colony, and this elegant city still contains many grand buildings from those days. The main attraction is the excellent **Sovereign Hill** historical park, a re-creation of the gold rush era. Other sights are the Ballarat Wildlife Park and Ballarat Fine Art Gallery.

www.visitballarat.com.au

✚ 137 D5

Sovereign Hill

✉ Bradshaw Street ☎ (03) 5337 1100 🕓 Daily 10–5. Closed 25 Dec ✋ Expensive

DANDENONG RANGES

Just 40km (25 miles) east of Melbourne are the delightful Dandenong Ranges – cool, moist hills cloaked with eucalypts and rainforest. Their many attractions include Puffing Billy, a quaint steam train which runs between Belgrave and Gembrook, and the William Ricketts Sanctuary, an unusual park featuring Aboriginal-themed sculptures.

www.parkweb.vic.gov.au
www.yarrarangestourism.com
✚ 137 D5 🚋 Upper Ferntree Gully or Belgrave
ℹ Visitor Centre ✉ 1211 Burwood Highway, Upper Ferntree Gully ☎ 1800 645 505 or (03) 9758 7522 🕐 Daily 9–5. Closed Good Fri, 25 Dec

GREAT OCEAN ROAD
See pages 30–31.

PHILLIP ISLAND
This scenic island, linked by bridge to the mainland, is famous for its nightly Penguin Parade – tiny fairy penguins waddling ashore to their burrows. The site of the parade and its visitor centre at

Summerland Beach are part of the **Phillip Island Nature Park,** which incorporates the island's Koala Conservation Centre (near the main town of Cowes), the ideal place to meet these cuddly marsupials.

www.visitphillipisland.com
www.penguins.org.au
➕ 137 E5

ℹ Visitor Information Centre
✉ 895 Phillip Island Tourist Road, Newhaven ☎ 1300 366 422 or (03) 5956 7447 🕐 Daily 9–5
Phillip Island Nature Park
☎ (03) 5951 2800 🕐 Koala Centre: daily 10–5.30. Penguin Centre: daily from 10am 🖐 Moderate 🚌 From Melbourne

WILSONS PROMONTORY NATIONAL PARK

The spectacular 'Prom' forms the Australian mainland's most southerly point. This is one of Victoria's most popular national parks, offering beaches and superb coastal scenery, rainforests, well-marked hiking trails, and a wide range of flora and fauna.

www.parkweb.vic.gov.au
➕ 137 E6 🖐 Inexpensive
ℹ Visitor Centre ✉ Tidal River
☎ (03) 5680 9555 🕐 Daily from 8.30am

Hobart

Tasmania's capital is one of Australia's most pleasant settlements. The small city of Hobart, on the River Derwent, is full of old colonial buildings; walking is the best way to appreciate the historic atmosphere. While here, take a river cruise and a trip to Mount Wellington (1,270m/4,167ft), which dominates the city – the view is sensational.
www.discovertasmania.com.au
✚ 137 F6

BATTERY POINT

With its charming mid-19th-century cottages and houses, craft and antiques shops and quaint

streets like Arthur's Circus, this inner city 'village' is Hobart's showpiece. Highlights are the **Narryna Heritage Museum** and the 1818 Signal Station and military base from which the suburb takes its name.

Narryna Heritage Museum
✉ 103 Hampden Road ☎ (03) 6234 2791 🕐 Mon–Fri 10.30–5, Sat–Sun 2–5. Closed Good Fri, Anzac Day, 25 Dec 🖐 Inexpensive

ROYAL TASMANIAN BOTANICAL GARDENS

These gardens, set high overlooking the river and full of native and exotic plants, form part of the large area of parkland known as the Queens Domain. They include a Conservatory, a Tropical Glasshouse and a museum of botany and horticulture.

www.rtbg.tas.gov.au

✉ Queens Domain ☎ (03) 6236 3075 ⊙ Daily from 8am ♿ Free general admission 🍴 Restaurant ($$)

SALAMANCA PLACE

This delightful old dockside street is lined with sandstone warehouses converted into restaurants and arts and crafts shops, and is the venue for Hobart's lively Saturday market. Antarctic Adventure, in neighbouring Salamanca Square, is well worth a visit, and nearby Sullivans Cove is where the first settlers landed in 1804.

www.salamanca.com.au

✉ Salamanca Place ⓐ Markets: Sat 8.30–3 ♿ Free 🍴 Many cafés and restaurants ($–$$$)

TASMANIAN MUSEUM AND ART GALLERY

Hobart's Tasmanian Museum contains some fine and varied exhibits, particularly on Australian mammals, convict history and the Indigenous Tasmanians. The attached art gallery holds a good collection of colonial art. An ideal place to discover the island's history.

www.tmag.tas.gov.au

✉ 40 Macquarie Street ☎ (03) 6211 4177 ⓐ Daily 10–5. Closed Good Fri, 25 Dec and Anzac Day ♿ Free

What to See in Tasmania

FREYCINET PENINSULA

Tasmania's east coast is renowned for beautiful scenery, none of which surpasses that of **Freycinet National Park** with its sandy white beaches, granite peaks and abundance of flora, birds and animals. The park is reached via the fishing settlement of Coles Bay. The town of Bicheno has more lovely beaches, great diving, a Sealife Centre and wildlife park.

www.dpiwe.tas.gov.au

✚ 137 F6 🚌 Tassie Link to Bicheno or Coles Bay ℹ Visitor Centre
✉ Freycinet Drive, Freycinet NP ☎ (03) 6256 7000 ⓐ Daily 8–6; winter 8–5

LAUNCESTON

Tasmania's second city, situated on the Tamar River and founded in 1805 (a year after Hobart), has retained many of its old buildings, which can be viewed on a self-guided walk around town. There are pleasant parks and reserves – a visit to the spectacular Cataract Gorge Reserve is recommended. The Queen Victoria Museum and Art Gallery, located at two sites (city centre and across the river at Inveresk) is also worth a visit.

The Launceston region is rich in historic houses and wineries.

www.discovertasmania.com.au

➕ 137 F6 🚌 or ✈ Launceston
ℹ Information Centre ✉ 12–16 St John Street ☎ (03) 6336 3133
🕐 Mon–Fri 9–5, Sat 9–3, Sun 9–12

THE MIDLANDS

The Midlands Highway, running for 200km (124 miles) between
Hobart and Launceston, passes through charming and historic
towns. Oatlands is full of atmospheric old buildings such as the
Court House, while, further north, picturesque Ross is famous for
its 1836 bridge and contains the **Tasmanian Wool Centre**,
devoted to the state's extensive wool industry.

➕ 137 F6

Tasmanian Wool Centre

✉ Church Street, Ross ☎ (03) 6381 5466 🕐 Daily 9–5 ✋ Inexpensive
🚌 Tasmanian Redline from Hobart

PORT ARTHUR AND THE TASMAN PENINSULA

Established as a far-flung penal settlement for the worst convict offenders in 1830, Port Arthur has over 30 ruins and historic sites, an excellent museum, and the settlement's poignant burial ground, the Isle of the Dead.

The surrounding Tasman Peninsula has magnificent scenery on the east coast, the Tasmanian Devil Park with an excellent wildlife collection, and the scenic Bush Mill Steam Railway.

www.portarthur.org.au

✚ 137 F6 ✉ Port Arthur Historic Site ☎ 1800 659 101 or (03) 6251 2300 ⏱ Daily 8.30–dusk

✋ Expensive; includes cruise and guided walk 🚌 Tassie Link from Hobart

STRAHAN

The lightly populated west coast is a region of wild coastline, rivers and forest lands. From the waterside village of Strahan (pronounced 'Strawn') you can go fishing, take a scenic flight, and cruise Macquarie Harbour – once the site of the brutal Sarah Island penal settlement – and the pristine Gordon River, part of the World Heritage-listed Franklin-Gordon Wild Rivers National Park. In town, the **Strahan Visitor Centre** provides a fascinating lesson in local history.

✚ 137 F5

Strahan Visitor Centre

✉ The Esplanade ☎ (03) 6471 7622 ⏱ Daily 10–6 ✋ Inexpensive 🚌 Tassie Link to Strahan

TASMANIA'S WORLD HERITAGE AREA

See pages 38–39.

South Australia and the Northern Territory

Founded in 1836 and settled by non-convicts, South Australia has an extraordinary range of scenery. There are fertile farming and wine-producing regions outside Adeliade in the south, but the majority of the land is taken up by the arid deserts and peaks of the Outback.

Originally part of South Australia, the sparsely populated Northern Territory is still real frontier country. Almost half of the population, a large proportion of which are Aboriginal people, lives in cosmopolitan Darwin. From the tropical 'Top End' to the desert lands of the 'Red Centre' around Alice Springs, the Northern Territory is endlessly fascinating, with superb natural attractions like Kakadu and Uluṟu.

The 2,979km (1,861 miles) between Adelaide and Darwin is now connected by the famous Ghan train, which takes two nights to cover the distance.

www.southaustralia.com
www.travelnt.com

Adelaide

South Australia's capital was first settled in December 1836, when HMS *Buffalo* docked at Glenelg with her 'cargo' of free settlers. Unlike many Australian cities, Adelaide was planned – Englishman Colonel William Light was responsible for the grid of city-centre streets. Adelaide was once known as the 'City of Churches' and for its conservative citizens, but today the 1.1 million population enjoys an enviable lifestyle and a Mediterranean climate.

Surrounded by large areas of parkland, and with the Adelaide Hills forming a splendid backdrop, Adelaide's compact and mostly flat city centre is a delightful place to explore; there are many old buildings, relatively little traffic, and a sense of calm which is rare in urban environments. This elegant city is famous for its café and restaurant scene, as well as for a thriving artistic and cultural life. The ideal time to be here is during the biennial (every even-numbered year), internationally acclaimed Adelaide Festival of Arts, when the city comes alive with everything from classical music concerts to outrageous fringe theatre.

In addition to visiting the museums and attractions detailed below, you should take a cruise on the placid and scenic River Torrens, which passes through the city. Within the metropolitan area, you can also visit the charming seaside suburb of Glenelg, where the first settlers landed in 1836 – it can be reached by an enjoyable tram ride from the city centre. The historic settlement of Port Adelaide was once the city's harbour town, but now concentrates on its heritage attractions, including the South Australian Maritime Museum and the National Railway Museum complex, the largest of its kind in the country.

www.adelaide.southaustralia.com

🚩 136 D3

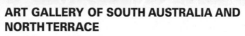

ART GALLERY OF SOUTH AUSTRALIA AND NORTH TERRACE

A stroll down North Terrace, Adelaide's grandest avenue, is the best way to see the city's historic buildings, several of which are open to the public. At the western end are the Adelaide Casino in a restored 1920s railway station, Old Parliament House, and the latter's neighbouring, much more impressive successor. East of King William Street lie the South Australian Museum, the Art Gallery of South Australia, and 1840s Ayers House, former home of Sir Henry Ayers, who was seven times Premier of South Australia and the inspiration behind the naming of Ayers Rock.

www.artgallery.sa.gov.au

✉ Art Gallery of South Australia: North Terrace ☎ (08) 8207 7000 🕐 Daily 10–5. Closed Good Fri am, 25 Dec 💷 Free general admission 🍴 Art Gallery Café ($–$$) 🚌 City Loop ❓ Free guided tours at regular intervals

GLENELG

Take the vintage tram from Victoria Square in the city to this popular seaside suburb where you can soak up the history and have a relaxed lunch in one of the many excellent eating establishments. Walk the pier and be sure to check out the replica of the HMS *Buffalo*, where there is an interesting museum and a popular family restaurant.

✉ Glenelg Visitor Centre, Foreshore ☎ (08) 8294 5833 ⏰ Mon–Fri 9–5, Sat–Sun 10–3 ✋ Free 🚌 Glenelg tram or 138 bus

SOUTH AUSTRALIAN MUSEUM

In addition to the usual natural history and general ethnographic and anthropological displays, this better-than-average museum has an internationally acclaimed collection of Aboriginal Australian artefacts. Another highlight is the large Pacific Cultures exhibit.

www.samuseum.sa.gov.au

✉ North Terrace ☎ (08) 8207 7500 ⏰ Daily 10–5. Closed Good Fri, 25 Dec ✋ Free 🚌 City Loop

TANDANYA NATIONAL ABORIGINAL CULTURAL INSTITUTE

This illuminating Aboriginal centre is one of a few of its kind in Australia. Including galleries with high-quality changing art exhibitions, workshops, and an area for dance and other performing arts, Tandanya (the local Aboriginal name for the Adelaide region) is a must for visitors. The centre has a shop selling gifts and a variety of good Aboriginal-made items.

www.tandanya.com.au

✉ 253 Grenfell Street ☎ (08) 8224 3200 ⏰ Daily 10–5 ✋ Inexpensive 🚌 City Loop

What to See in South Australia

ADELAIDE HILLS

Just 20 minutes east of the city, this region of hills, bushland, vineyards and picturesque small towns is a popular weekend destination. Attractions include good views from the summit of Mount Lofty, botanic gardens, the acclaimed National Motor Museum at Birdwood, and Warrawong Earth Sanctuary – an important wildlife reserve. The German-style main town of Hahndorf has fine artworks in the Hahndorf Academy.

www.visitadelaidehills.com.au

✚ 136 D3 🚌 From Adelaide

ℹ️ Visitor Information Centre ✉ 41 Main Street, Hahndorf ☎ (08) 8388 1185

🕐 Mon–Fri 9–5, Sat–Sun 10–4

BAROSSA VALLEY

The wine-producing area of the Barossa was settled in the 1830s by Silesians and Prussians, and this picturesque valley is characterised by distinctive European architecture, traditions and cuisine. You can visit some of the 50 or so wineries, and enjoy the ambience of towns and villages like Tanunda, Bethany, Lyndoch and Angaston.

www.barossa-region.org

🚏 136 D3 🚌 or 🚆 From Adelaide

ℹ️ Barossa Wine and Visitor Information Centre ✉️ 66–68 Murray Street, Tanunda ☎️ 1300 852 982 or (08) 8563 0600 🕐 Mon–Fri 9–5, Sat–Sun 10–4. Closed Good Fri, 25 Dec

FLINDERS RANGES NATIONAL PARK

A rugged desert mountain chain containing one of the most ancient landscapes on earth. Plenty of wildlife can be found, while there are several good hikes that allow you to see the diverse plantlife. The highlights of the Park are Wilpena Pound, an enormous 80sq km (30 sq mile) elevated amphitheatre surrounded by sheer cliffs, and St Mary's Peak (1,165m/3,822ft), a challenging walk for experienced hikers. The area is rich in Aboriginal art.

www.environment.sa.gov.au

✚ 136 C3 ✋ Inexpensive 🚌 or ✖ From Adelaide 🛈 Wilpena Pound Visitor Centre ☎ (08) 8648 0048 ⏲ Daily 8–6

KANGAROO ISLAND

Australia's third largest island is a relaxed place with spectacular scenery, remarkable wildlife, and pleasant small towns like the main settlement of Kingscote. There are rugged cliffs and sandy beaches; a large part of the island is within Flinders Chase National Park, domain of kangaroos, koalas and prolific birdlife; and you can view Australian sea lions from close quarters at Seal Bay Conservation Park.

www.tourkangarooisland.com.au

➕ 136 D3 ✈ From Adelaide ⛴ From Cape Jervis

ℹ Kangaroo Island Gateway Visitor Centre ✉ Howard Drive, Pennesaw ☎ 1800 811 080 or (08) 8553 1185 🕐 Mon–Fri 9–5, Sat–Sun 10–4. Closed 25 Dec

Darwin

The Northern Territory's capital and largest city was founded in 1869. Situated closer to Asia than to any major Australian cities, it has a multicultural population of about 108,000. Darwin was bombed by the Japanese during World War II, and suffered another catastrophe in 1974, when Cyclone Tracy virtually flattened the city. Located on vast Darwin Harbour (on which a cruise is highly recommended), this tropical, modern settlement is a laid-back place. Few reminders of Darwin's history remain, but you can visit the 1883 Fannie Bay Gaol and take a historical walk around the city centre.

www.travelnt.com ✚ 134 B1

DARWIN WHARF PRECINCT

This busy waterfront complex includes shops, cafés and restaurants, and you can go fishing or take a boat excursion from the wharf. The Australian Pearling Exhibition is here, as are the Indo Pacific Marine – an award-winning education and environment centre – and the Deckchair Outdoor Cinema.

✉ Stokes Hill Wharf ☎ (08) 8981 4268 🕐 Precinct: daily. Attractions: 10–5 👋 Attractions: moderate

GEORGE BROWN DARWIN BOTANIC GARDENS

Containing the southern hemisphere's most extensive collection of tropical palms, an orchid farm, a rainforest area and wetlands flora, Darwin's gardens are a delightful place in which to relax or escape the heat.

✉ Geranium Street, The Gardens ☎ (08) 8981 1958 ◑ Daily 7–7 ✋ Free

MINDIL BEACH

Although swimming is not recommended due to box jellyfish, sharks and crocodiles, this pleasant beach offers a park, wonderful sunsets, Darwin's casino and the famous **Mindil Beach Sunset Markets**).

Mindil Beach Sunset Markets
🕒 Apr–Oct Thu 5–10, Sun 4–9

MUSEUM AND ART GALLERY OF THE NORTHERN TERRITORY

This well-planned, modern complex includes the Maritime Museum, a good collection of Aboriginal and Australian art, and displays on local and military history, natural science and Cyclone Tracy (➤ 104). There is a café in the museum.
www.magnt.nt.gov.au
✉ Conacher Street, Bullocky Point ☎ (08) 8999 8201 🕒 Mon–Fri 9–5, Sat–Sun 10–5. Closed Good Fri, 25 Dec ✋ Free

What to See in the Northern Territory

ALICE SPRINGS

Affectionately known as 'The Alice', this unpretentious Outback town at the heart of the continent was founded as a remote Overland Telegraph station in 1871. Alice Springs is full of attractions: you can take a camel ride, or visit the Old Telegraph Station, the Royal Flying Doctor Service base, a variety of museums and the fascinating Aboriginal Art and Culture Centre.

Nearby, the rugged MacDonnell Ranges contain steep gorges, nature reserves, historic settlements and homesteads, ancient Aboriginal sites, national parks and Palm Valley, where 3,000 rare and ancient palm trees grow.

www.centralaustraliantourism.com

✚ 134 E2 🚉 The Ghan from Darwin, Adelaide and Sydney ✈ Alice Springs ⓘ Central Australian Tourism Industry Association ✉ 60 Gregory Terrace ☎ 1800 645 199 or (08) 8952 5800 🕒 Mon–Fri 8.30–5.30, Sat–Sun 9–4

DEVIL'S MARBLES CONSERVATION RESERVE

Beside the Stuart Highway to the south of Tennant Creek, these huge, curiously eroded granite boulders are significant in Aboriginal mythology – legend says they are the eggs of the Rainbow Serpent.

www.tennantcreektourism.com.au

✚ 134 D2 ⓘ Tennant Creek Regional Tourist Association ✉ Peko Road ☎ (08) 8962 3388 🕒 Generally Mon–Fri 9–5, Sat 9–12

KAKADU NATIONAL PARK

See pages 32–33.

KATHERINE AND NITMILUK NATIONAL PARK

Katherine, the Territory's third largest settlement, is a pleasant town with a museum, a nature reserve and some historic buildings. The main attraction is nearby Nitmiluk (Katherine Gorge) National Park, with 13 dramatic sandstone gorges. The best way to appreciate Nitmiluk is by taking a cruise on the Katherine River.
www.krta.com.au

➕ 134 B2 🚆 The Ghan from Darwin and Alice Springs ✈ Katherine
ℹ Katherine Region Tourist Association ✉ Lindsay Street, Katherine
☎ 1800 653 142 or (08) 8972 3249 🕐 Mon–Fri 8.30–5, Sat–Sun 9–2

ULURU–KATA TJUTA NATIONAL PARK

See pages 40–41.

WATARRKA NATIONAL PARK

This remote desert park, north of Uluru, is famous for Kings Canyon – a spectacular sandstone gorge with walls over 200m (655ft) high. Visitors can explore lush waterholes, wonder at the strangely weathered rocks of the Lost City, and take a challenging bushwalk. There is a wide variety of flora and fauna, including some extraordinary ancient palm trees.
www.nt.gov.au/ipe/pwcnt

➕ 134 E1 ✋ Free
🚫 None ℹ Central Australian Tourism Association
✉ 60 Gregory Terrace, Alice Springs ☎ 1800 645 199 or (08) 8952 5800

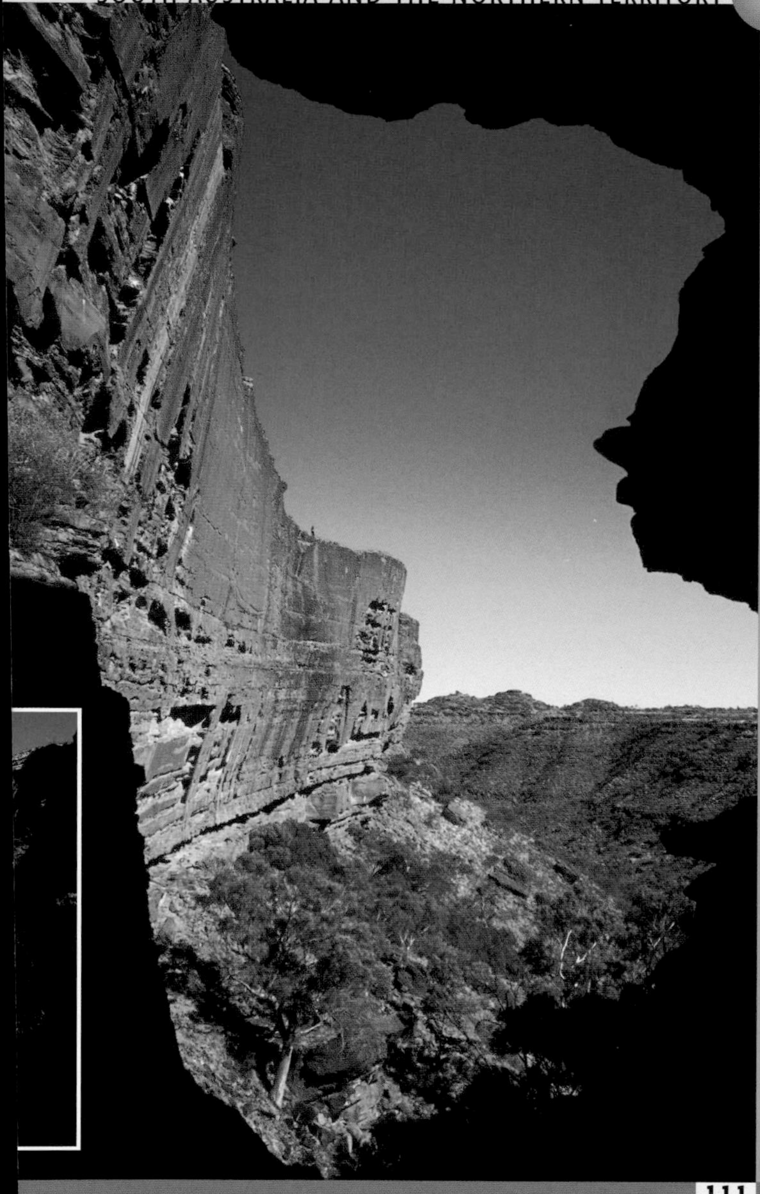

Darwin to Litchfield National Park

This drive makes an easy day trip and takes in several attractions outside Darwin, plus a superb national park.

From Darwin's centre, follow the signs to the Stuart Highway and Winnellie.

In the outer suburb of Winnellie, the Australian Aviation Heritage Centre has a good collection of aircraft, including a massive B-52 bomber.

Continue south on the Highway.

Darwin Crocodile Farm, 40km (25 miles) south of Darwin, has over 10,000 saltwater and freshwater crocodiles. This farm and research centre is the ideal place to inspect the most fearsome of reptiles.

Continue south, then take the Berry Springs turn-off.

Berry Springs has two major attractions – the large Territory Wildlife Park, with its excellent collection of native fauna, and the nearby Berry Springs Nature Park, a great spot for a swim or a barbecue.

Return to the Stuart Highway and drive south. Take the Batchelor turn-off.

The small settlement of Batchelor, once a dormitory town for workers at the nearby Rum Jungle uranium field, is best known as the gateway to Litchfield National Park.

Continue for another 21km (13 miles) into the park.

Litchfield National Park, a rugged yet delightful reserve, was little known before the mid-1980s, as it was on private land. Today, visitors come here to enjoy the spectacular waterfalls, refreshing swimming holes, hiking trails and superb views of the region. Other highlights include a small 1930s pioneers' homestead; tall 'magnetic' termite mounds, so called because they always face north–south; and the Lost City, an area of curious sandstone pillars.

Return to Darwin via Batchelor and the Stuart Highway.

Distance 280km (174 miles)
Time A full day is necessary
Start/end point Central Darwin
✛ 134 B1
Lunch Territory Wildlife Park ($)
✉ Cox Peninsula Road, Berry Springs
☎ (08) 8988 7200

Western Australia

Western Australia takes up almost a third of the continent, but is home to just under 2 million people, the vast majority living in Perth and Fremantle. Much of the terrain is arid and used for little more than cattle farming and mining. The discovery of gold in the southeast in the 1890s initially brought prosperity, and modern Western Australia has boomed because of the extraordinary wealth created by iron ore mining in particular.

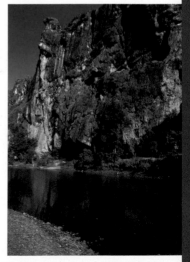

Natural wonders here are remarkable: tall forests in the southwest; a coastline of white sandy beaches and rugged cliffs; extraordinary wildlife, including marsupials like the numbat and quokka, unique to the state; and the dramatic rock formations of the Kimberley in the far north. Many of the southern wild flowers are also found nowhere else in Australia. Although there is much to see, distances are vast – flying is best option for getting around.
www.westernaustralia.com

Perth

Founded in 1829 by free settlers, and initially known as the Swan River Colony, Perth began life as an incredibly isolated outpost of Sydney and the eastern part of the continent. This isolation continues today. Despite its prosperity and cosmopolitan ambience, Perth is the world's most remote city – separated from the east by the desert lands of the Nullarbor Plain, with the nearest large centre, Adelaide, over 2,700km (1,680 miles) away. Much of Perth's charm is due to its location. The city is in a delightful setting on the broad Swan River; some of Australia's best urban beaches lie to the west; and the metropolitan area is backed by the low hills of the Darling Range to the east. The climate is warm and sunny, the generally rather affluent lifestyle is enviable, and the atmosphere is very relaxed for a state capital.

Perth's small and mostly modern city centre, much of which was reconstructed during the 1980s with the proceeds of the state's mineral wealth, offers quite a few attractions of its own. There are historic buildings, many parks and gardens, excellent restaurants and some good nightlife venues. But the true delights of this western capital lie a little beyond the city centre.

Perth is seen at its best from the white sandy beaches of Cottesloe and Scarborough, and on cruises up the Swan River to the vineyards of the fertile Avon Valley. Another highlight is the ferry trip to the atmospheric port town of Fremantle (➤ 120), 19km (12 miles) downstream.

www.cityofperth.wa.gov.au 🚼 132 F2

KINGS PARK

Overlooking the city and the Swan River, this popular 400ha (990-acre) reserve consists largely of unspoiled bushland, with colourful wild flowers and prolific birdlife. It also includes the Western Australian Botanic Garden and the State War Memorial. The best way to explore is by renting a bike; or joining a walking tour.

✉ Off Fraser Avenue ☎ (08) 9480 3600 🕐 Daily 🖐 Free 🍽 Restaurants ($–$$) 🚌 33 or Perth Tram bus ❓ Free guided walks daily at 10am and 2pm, departing from opposite Visitor Information Centre

ST GEORGE'S TERRACE

A walk along Perth's grandest avenue is the ideal way to see some of the city's historic buildings. Near Pier Street you will find the 1850s Deanery, the neo-Gothic St George's Cathedral, and Government House (1864). Closer to Kings Park are the 1850s Old Perth Boys' School, now owned by the National Trust and also containing a gift shop and café, and the Cloisters, a former collegiate school.

✉ St George's Terrace ⏰ Some buildings open weekdays 9–5
✋ Free 🚌 Central Area Transit bus

WESTERN AUSTRALIAN MUSEUM

Incorporating Perth's original 1850s gaol and an early settler's cottage, this is the state's largest and most comprehensive museum. There are displays on Western Australian mammals, birds and marine life, but the highlight is the Aboriginal gallery. While in this northern city area, visit the Art Gallery of Western Australia, on nearby James Street.

www.museum.wa.gov.au
✉ James Street Mall ☎ (08) 9427 2700 ⏰ Daily 9.30–5. Closed Good Fri, 25 Dec, 1 Jan ✋ Donation (moderate for special exhibitions)
🍴 Coffee shop ($) 🚌 Central Area Transit bus

What to See in Western Australia

ALBANY

Now a scenic holiday resort, Albany was Western Australia's first settlement. Founded three years before Perth, the town developed into a port and whaling centre. The old whaling station is now the fascinating Whale World museum, and there is whale watching here from August to October. The town contains the 1850s Residency and Old Gaol, both now museums. The coastline and beaches are spectacular, as is the rugged mountain country of Stirling Range National Park, which lies 100km (62 miles) inland.

www.albanytourist.com.au

➕ 132 F3 ✈ Albany
ℹ Albany Visitor Centre ✉ Old Railway Station, Proudlove Parade
☎ (08) 9841 1088 🕐 Daily 9–5

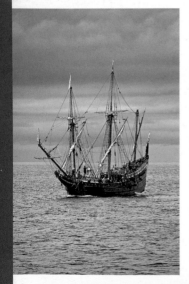

FREMANTLE

Perth's seaport is reached by train or a short boat trip down the Swan River. Fremantle's harbourside location, delightful old buildings and quaint streets make it irresistible. Don't miss the informative Western Australian Maritime Museum, the Fremantle Motor Museum, the markets, the Round House and the austere Fremantle Prison.

www.fremantle.com

➕ 132 F2 🚊 or 🚢 Fremantle
ℹ Fremantle Tourist Bureau ✉ Town Hall, Kings Square ☎ (08) 9431 7878
🕐 Mon–Fri 9–5, Sat 10–3

KALGOORLIE-BOULDER

Prospectors flocked to this barren Outback region, 600km (372 miles) east of Perth, when rich gold deposits were discovered near Kalgoorlie in 1893. The area still produces nickel and gold. The city of Kalgoorlie and its smaller neighbour, Boulder, contain fine old buildings, the Australian Prospectors and Miners Hall of Fame, at the Hannans North Mine complex, and a Royal Flying Doctor base. The well-preserved ghost town of Coolgardie is also worth a visit.

www.kalgoorlie.com

✚ 132 E4 🚋 Prospector from Perth ✈ Kalgoorlie
ℹ Kalgoorlie Goldfields Visitor Centre ✉ 250 Hannan Street, Kalgoorlie
☎ (08) 9021 1966 🕓 Mon–Fri 8.30–5, Sat–Sun 9–5. Closed 25 Dec

THE KIMBERLEY

See pages 34–35.

MARGARET RIVER

Some of Australia's best wines are produced around this picturesque town, 280km (174 miles) south of Perth, in over 50 wineries, including the excellent Vasse Felix and Leeuwin Estate. You can sample the wines produced at many of them. The area has wonderful beaches, great surfing and bushwalking along the cliffs of nearby Leeuwin-Naturaliste National Park. The Margaret River township has galleries, craft shops and fine restaurants.

www.margaretriver.com

🚇 132 F2 🚌 The Australind to Bunbury, then a bus

ℹ Margaret River Tourist Bureau ✉ 100 Bussell Highway, Margaret River ☎ (08) 9757 2911

🕐 Daily 9–5

NAMBUNG NATIONAL PARK AND THE PINNACLES

This coastal national park to the north of Perth bristles with
thousands of limestone pillars and needles reaching up to 6m
(19ft) in height. Early Dutch seafarers believed they had sighted a
ruined city, but the Pinnacles are actually the eroded remnants of a
former thick bed of limestone. The area has good beaches.
www.calm.wa.gov.au

➕ 132 E2 ✉ Nambung National Park, via Cervantes ☎ (08) 9652 7043
🕐 Daily 🖐 Inexpensive 🚌 None

PEMBERTON

A visit to the small town of Pemberton, at the heart of the
southwest's 'Tall Timber Country', reveals a very different aspect of
Western Australia. Giant 400-year-old hardwood trees – jarrah, karri
and marri – tower 100m (330ft) above the dense undergrowth.
Ride the Pemberton Tramway through the forests and visit the
local sawmill and a museum.
www.pembertontourist.com.au

➕ 132 F2 🚉 The Australind to Bunbury, then a bus
ℹ Pemberton Visitor Centre ✉ Brockman Street ☎ (08) 9776 1133
🕐 Daily 9–5. Closed 25 Dec

ROTTNEST ISLAND

This idyllic island lies just 90 minutes by ferry or 15 minutes by air from Perth. First discovered by Dutch seafarers in the 17th century and mistakenly named 'rat's nest' for the quokkas (small marsupials that still roam the island), Rottnest has almost 40km (25 miles) of extraordinarily white beaches, crystal-clear waters that are perfect for fishing, diving and snorkelling, and a relaxed, car-free atmosphere.

www.rottnest.wa.gov.au

✚ 132 F2 🚢 From Perth, Fremantle or Hillarys Boat Harbour 🖐 Ferry fare: expensive (includes entrance fee to island)

ℹ️ Rottnest Island Visitor Centre ✉️ Thomson Bay

☎ (08) 9372 9732 🕐 Daily 8.30–5

SHARK BAY

With islands and 1,500km (930 miles) of indented coastline, the World Heritage Site of Shark Bay, on the state's mid-north coast, is a marine wonderland. This vast inlet is

famous for Monkey Mia beach, where wild dolphins come close to the shore to be hand fed. Visit dazzlingly white Shell Beach and François Peron National Park, and see Hamelin Pool's stromatolites, some of the world's oldest living organisms.

www.sharkbay.asn.au

✚ 132 D2 🖐 Inexpensive

❌ Denham ℹ️ Shark Bay Tourist Bureau ✉️ 71 Knight Terrace, Denham ☎ (08) 9948 1253

🕐 Daily 9–5

WAVE ROCK

This stunning rock formation is one of Western Australia's
strangest natural wonders. Wave Rock is a 14m-high (46ft) granite
wall, more than 100m (330ft) long, which has been eroded over
almost 3,000 million years into the shape of a breaking wave.
Other curious (and curiously named) formations in the area include
the Breakers and the Hippo's Yawn, and you can also look at
Aboriginal hand paintings at Mulkas Cave.

www.waverock.com.au

🕂 132 F3 ✋ Free 🚌 None

🛈 Hyden Tourist Centre ✉ Wave Rock ☎ (08) 9880 5182 🕐 Daily 9–5 or 6

a drive south of Perth

Taking in beautiful coastal scenery, this drive can just about be accomplished in a day – or you might want to stay overnight to fully appreciate the area.

Leave Perth via the Stirling Highway, then follow Cockburn Road and Patterson Road to Rockingham.

Make a brief stop at Rockingham, an attractive seaside resort offering excellent beaches and the chance to see fairy penguins at Penguin Island.

Continue south on the Mandurah Road.

Located on the coast at the mouth of idyllic Peel Inlet, Mandurah is the perfect spot for swimming, fishing and boating. There is a wildlife park, a miniature village, and swimming with dolphins in summer.

Continue south on the Old Coast Road.

Yalgorup National Park offers a peaceful environment of swamps, lakes, dunes and woodland. Birdwatchers should look out for some of the 100 or so species of waterbird that frequent the area.

Continue south.

The popular seaside resort of Bunbury has good beaches and a harbour, and you might well see dolphins at Koombana Beach, where the Dolphin Discovery Centre is located. You can drive further south to see the tall 400-year-old trees of the Tuart Forest National Park. If you wish to stay in the area overnight, continue to Busselton and Margaret River (➤ 122).

Head back towards Perth on the fast South Western Highway.

Returning to Perth, stop at the historic town of Armadale (History House Museum), 30km (18 miles) from the city, the Araluen Botanic Park at Roleystone, and Cohunu Koala Park at Gosnells.

Continue on to Perth.

Distance 360km (224 miles) **Time** A full day or more
Start/end point Central Perth ✚ 132 F2
Lunch Benesse Cafe ($) ✉ 83 Victoria Street, Bunbury
☎ (08) 9791 4030

Index

Acknowledgements

The Automobile Association would like to thank the following photographers, companies and picture libraries for their assistance in the preparation of this book.

Abbreviations for the picture credits are as follows – (t) top; (b) bottom; (c) centre; (l) left; (r) right; (AA) AA World Travel Library; Aust: Australian; SA: South Australia; WA: Western Australia; NT: Northern Territory; Qld: Queensland; Vic: Victoria, NT: Northern Territory; Aust TC: Australian Tourist Commission; WATC: Western Australia Tourist Commission; SATC: South Australia Touist Commission

4l Milsons Point in Sydney, AA/ M Langford; **4c** Great Barrier Reef, Australian Tourist Commission; **4r** Walkers near Cradle Mountain, Australian Tourist Commission; **5l** Sydney, AA/S Day; **5r** People on horseback, AA/B Bachman; **6/7** Milsons Point in Sydney, AA/ M Langford; **10** The National Tennis Centre in Melbourne, AA/ B Bachman; **10/11** Fringe Festival in Melbourne, AA/B Bachman; **12/13** Melaleuca Airstrip, AA/ M Cawood; **14** The Ghan train, AA/ M Langford; **15** Road sign, AA /M Langford; **20/21** Great Barrier Reef, Australian Tourist Commission; **22** Canyoning, AA/S Richmond; **22/23** Blue Mountains, AA/P Kenward; **24/25t** Kuranda, AA/A Belcher; **24/25** Port Douglas, AA/A Belcher; **25** Birdworld in Kuranda, AA/A Belcher; **26** Wet 'n' Wild Water World, AA/A Belcher; **26/27** Warner Brothers Movie World, AA/A Belcher; **27** Currumbin Wildlife Sanctuary, AA/A Belcher; **28** Great Barrier Reef, Australian Tourist Commission; **28/29t** Divers, AA/A Belcher; **29** Townsville, AA/A Belcher; **30/31t** Great Ocean Road, AA/B Bachman; **30/31b** Twelve Apostles, Great Ocean Road, Australian Tourist Commission/David Simmons; **32** Kakadu National Park, AA/S Watkins; **32/3t** Kakadu National Park, AA/S Watkins; **32/33b** Nourlangie Rock art, AA/S Watkins; **34** The Kimberley, Australian Tourist Commission; **34/35** The Kimberley, AA/S Watkins; **36/37t** Sydney Opera House, AA/S Day; **36/37b** Sydney Harbour, AA/M Langford; **37** Sydney Opera House, Australian Tourist Commission; **38/39** Cradle Mountain, AA/S Richmond; **39** Mount Ossa, AA/S Richmond; **40/41** Ayers Rock, AA/S Richmond; **42/43** Walkers near Cradle Mountain, Australian Tourist Commission; **45** Hunter Valley, AA/S Day; **46/47t** Australian Museum AA/S Day; **46/47b** Darling Harbour, AA/S Day; **48** The Rocks, AA/M Langford; **48/49** The Rocks, AA/M Langford; **49** Sydney Harbour Bridge, AA/P Kenward; **50** Sydney Tower, AA/P Kenward; **51** Taronga Zoo, AA/S Day; **52** Australian National Botanic Gardens, AA/A Baker; **52/53** Australian War Memorial, AA/P Kenward; **54/55** Parliament House, AA/P Kenward; **55** Parliament House, AA/A Baker; **56/57** Lighthouse at Byron Bay, Australian Tourist Commission; **58t** Hunter Valley, AA/S Day; **58b** Hunter Valley, AA/S Day; **59** Kangaroo Valley, AA/P Kenward; **60/61** Mount Kosciuszko, AA/S Richmond; **61l** Moss Vale, AA/P Kenward; **61r** Morton National Park, AA/P Kenward; **62** Lady in sea, AA/A Belcher; **63** Noosa, AA/A Belcher; **65** Brisbane Botanic Gardens, AA/A Belcher; **66** Mount Coot-tha, AA/A Belcher; **66/67** South Bank, AA/A Belcher; **68** Charters Towers, AA/A Belcher; **69** Charters Towers, AA/A Belcher; **70** Fraser Island, AA/A Belcher; **70/71** Fraser Island, AA/A Belcher; **71** Lamington National Park, AA/A Belcher; **72** Noosa, AA/A Belcher; **72/73** Noosa Heads, AA/A Belcher; **73** Pelican, AA/A Belcher; **74/75t** Townsville, AA/A Belcher; **74/75b** Townsville, AA/A Belcher; **75** Whitsunday Islands, AA/ L K Stow; **76** View along Yarra River, AA/B Bachman; **77** St Kilda, AA/B Bachman; **78/79** Melbourne Cricket Ground, AA/B Bachman; **79** Melbourne Museum, AA/B Bachman; **80/81** Melbourne, AA/B Bachman; **81** National Gallery of Victoria, AA/A Baker; **82/83** St Kilda, AA/B Bachman; **83t** St Kilda, AA/B Bachman; **83b** St Kilda, AA/B Bachman; **84** Ballarat, AA/B Bachman; **84/85** Ballarat, AA/B Bachman; **85t** Dandenong Ranges, AA/B Bachman; **85b** Puffing Billy, AA/B Bachman; **86/87** Phillip Island, AA/B Bachman; **88** Hobart, AA/A Baker; **88/89** Hobart, AA/A Baker; **90/91** Freycinet National Park, AA/N Rains; **92** Launceston, AA/A Baker; **92/93** Cataract Gorge, AA/A Baker; **94** Port Arthur, AA; **95** Flinders Ranges National Park, AA/M Cawood; **96/97** Atrium of the Art Gallery of South Australia, Art Gallery of South Australia; **97** Front of the Art Gallery of South Australia, Art Gallery of South Australia; **98** Glenelg City in Adelaide in South Australia, South Australian Tourism Commission; **100** National Motor Museum in Birdwood in the Adelaide Hills, South Australia, South Australian Tourism Commission/Adelaide Hills Tourism/Adam Bruzzone; **100/1** View of the Adelaide Hills in South Australia, South Australian Tourism Commission/Adam Bruzzone; **101** Grant Burge Filsell Vineyard in Barossa, Grant Burge Wines Pty Ltd; **102** Flinders Ranges National Park, AA/M Cawood; **102/103** Flinders Ranges National Park, AA/M Cawood; **103** Kangaroo Island, South Australia Tourist Board; **104/105t** The Ghan arriving at Darwin Railway Station, Tourism NT/David Silva; **104/105b** Darwin Wharf Precinct, Tourism NT/ Peter Solness; **106/107t** George Brown Darwin Botanic Gardens, Tourism NT; **106/107b** Aerial of Mindil Beach, Tourism NT/Barry Skipsey; **108t** Alice Springs, AA/S Richmond; **108/109** Alice Springs, AA/S Richmond; **109** Devil's Marbles, AA/A Baker; **110/111** Kings Canyon, AA/S Richmond; **111** Kings Canyon, AA/ S Richmond; **112/113** The Tjaynera Falls, AA/S Watkins; **113** Litchfield National Park, AA/S Watkins; **114** Horse riders, Australian Tourist Commission; **115** The Kimberley, AA/S Watkins; **116/117t** Swan Bells viewing platform, AA/ M Langford; **116/117b** Perth, AA/ M Langford; **118/119** Kings Park, AA/M Langford; **120** Fremantle, AA/M Langford; **120/121** Kalgoorlie, AA/A Baker; **122t** Margaret River, AA/M Langford; **122b** Margaret River, AA/M Langford; **123** The Pinnacles, AA/A Baker; **124** Shell Beach, AA/A Belcher; **124/125** Wave Rock, Western Australia Tourism; **126/127** Bunbury, Western Australian Tourism Commission.

Every effort has been made to trace the copyright holders, and we apologise in advance for any accidental errors. We would be happy to apply the corrections in the following edition of this publication.

Maps

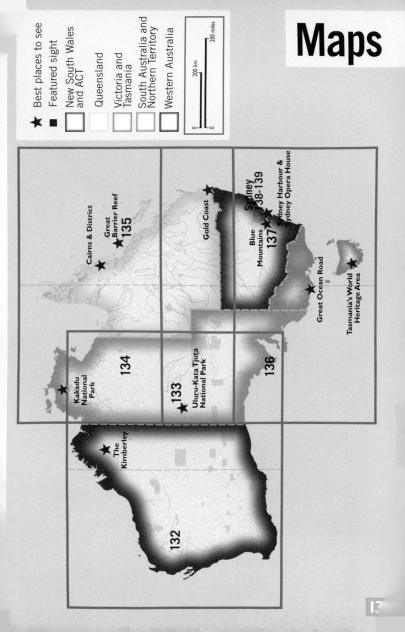

★ Best places to see
■ Featured sight

New South Wales and ACT

Queensland

Victoria and Tasmania

South Australia and Northern Territory

Western Australia

0   200 km
0   200 miles

The Kimberley ★

132

Kakadu National Park ★

134

133

Uluru-Kata Tjuta National Park ★

Cairns & District ★

Great Barrier Reef ★ 135

Gold Coast ★

Sydney ★ 138–139

Blue Mountains 137 ★

Sydney Harbour & Sydney Opera House ★

136

Great Ocean Road ★

Tasmania's World Heritage Area ★

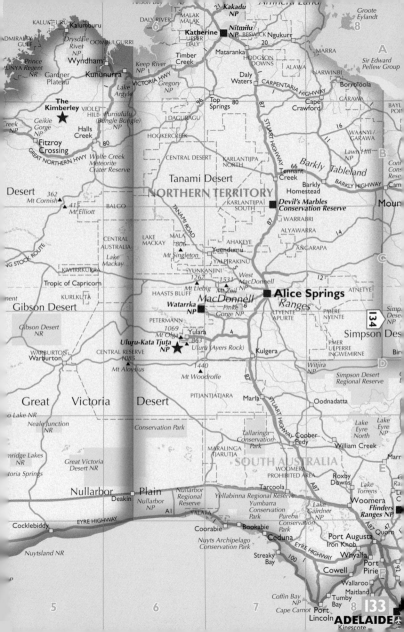

Badu Island
Prince of
Wales Island

Melville
Island
Cobourg
Pennisula
Croker
Island
Wessel
Islands

Bathurst Island
Van Diemen
Gulf
Elcho
Island

DARWIN · Howard Springs
Nhulunbuy
Cape Arnhem
Weipa

DELISSAVILLE WAGAIT
LARRAKIA
LITCHFIELD
NP
Adelaide
River
Jabiru
Arnhem Land
ARUKUN
Pon

Anson Bay
MALAK
MALAK
Kakadu
NP
Groote
Eylandt
PORMPURAAW/
EDWARD RIVER
Mu
Kan

DALY RIVER
Katherine
Nitmiluk
NP
BESWICK Ngukurr
Gulf of
Carpentaria

ULGURRI
UPPER
DALY
20
MARRA
Wallaby Island
KOWANYAMA
Mi
Ali

Keep River
NP
Timber
Creek
Mataranka
HODGSON
DOWNS
ALAWA
NARWINBI
Sir Edward
Pellew Group

Lake
Argyle
VICTORIA HWY
Gregory
NP
Daly
Waters
CARPENTARIA HIGHWAY
Borroloola
Mornington
Island
Staaten

rrungle Bungle)
DAGURAGU
Top
Springs
80
GARAWA
BAYLEY
POINT
Bentinck
Island
Karumba
Normanton

HOOKERCREEK
CENTRAL DESERT
KARLANTIJPA
NORTH
WAANYI/
GARAWA
DOOMADGEE
Burketown

Creek
rite
Reserve
Barkly
Tableland
Lawn Hill
NP
Connells Lagoon
Conservation
Reserve
Burke & Wills
Roadhouse

Tanami Desert
66
Tennant
Creek
Camooweal
Julia
Creek

NORTHERN TERRITORY
KARLANTIJPA
SOUTH
Devil's Marbles
Conservation Reserve
Barkly
Homestead
BARKLY HIGHWAY
Mount Isa
Cloncurry
LANDSBOROU

ALGO
TANAMI ROAD
LAKE
MACKAY
MALA
806
WARRABRI
ALYAWARRA
ANGARAPA
14
Boulia
LANDSBOR

ENTRAL
STRALIA
Lake
ackay
Mt Singleton
Yuendumu
YALPIRAKINU
12

YUUNKANJINI
1267
West
MacDonnell
NP
Alice Springs
ATNETYE
Diamantina
Gates NP
QUEENSLANE

HAASTS BLUFF
Mt Liebig
1531
Mt Zeil
MacDonnell
Ranges
PMERE
NYENTE
Simpson
Desert
NP
Bedourie

Watarrka
NP
Finke
Gorge NP
LTYENTE
APURTE
PMER
ULPERRE
INGWEMIRNE

PETERMANN
1069
Yulara
Uluru-Kata Tjuta
NP
Mt Olga
863
Uluru (Ayers Rock)
Kulgera
Simpson Desert
Birdsville

RAL RESERVE
1085
Mt Aloysius
1440
Mt Woodroffe
Witjira
NP
Simpson Desert
Regional Reserve
Goyder
Lagoon
Sturt
Stony
Desert

Desert
PITJANTJATJARA
Marla
STUART HIGHWAY
Oodnadatta
Innamincka
Regional
Reserve

Conservation Park
Tallaringa
Conservation
Park
Coober
Pedy
Lake
Eyre
North
Lake
Eyre
South
Innamincka
Strzelecki
Regional
Reserve
Strzelecki Desert

MARALINGA
TJARUTJA
William Creek
Marree
Gammon
Ranges NP

SOUTH AUSTRALIA
WOOMERA
PROHIBITED AREA
Roxby
Downs
booburra

A

oa Island
rn Island

Bamaga
Jardine River
NP

Iron Range NP

B

kan
NP   Port Stewart

Cape Melville NP

Lakefield
NP
HOPE VALE
ell and
Rivers NP   Cooktown

Daintree
81   Port Douglas
Kuranda   Green Island NP
Mareeba
Cairns
Atherton
er   Atherton   Wooroonooran NP
NP   Tableland   Mt   Innisfail
Bulleringa   Surprise   Tully
NP   Lumholtz
Georgetown   Undara   NP
Volcanic   Hinchinbrook
Island

C

Ingham

Barrier ★

Great   **Townsville**
Ayr
Great Basalt   Bowen
Wall NP   **Charters**   Hook Island NP
White Mountains   **Towers**   Collinsville   **Whitsunday**
DERS   HIGHWAY NP   Proserpine   **Islands**
Richmond   A6   Pentland   Eungella   Great Barrier
Hughenden   NP   Mackay   Reef Marine
   Sarina   Park

D

Beylando
Crossing   Moranbah
2   Winton   Dividing
Muttaburra   Clermont   Dysart
ladensburg   70   Great Keppel
NP   Goodedulla   Island
ochern   **Longreach**   A4   CAPRICORN   HIGHWAY   Emerald   NP   Yeppoon
NP   Isisford   Barcaldine   Alpha   Blackwater   **Rockhampton**
   Blackall   Moura   Mount   Gladstone
   Morgan
Welford   Tambo   **Carnarvon**   Biloela   Miriam Vale
NP   Idalia   **Gorge NP**   Expedition   Monto
Windorah   NP   NP   Bundaberg
Hell Hole   Augathella   Range   **Hervey Bay**
Gorge NP   Charleville   Murgon   **Maryborough**
   Roma   A2   Miles   *Fraser*
Quilpie   Kingaroy   *Island*
   Surat   Dalby   **Sunshine**
   Wyandra   Moonie   **Coast**
occundra   St George   Caboolture   *Moreton Island*
   Cunnamulla   49   Bollon   Millmerran   **Toowoomba**   Gatton   Redcliffe
hargomindah   Nindigully   Goondiwindi   **Ipswich**   **BRISBANE**
Currawinya   Hebel   *Lamington NP*   Southport
NP   Mungindi   Yetman   Lismore   **Gold Coast**
   Coolangatta

E

F

Wanaaring   Lightning Ridge   **137**   Garah   Moree   Tenterfield   *Washpool*   **Byron**
   38   NP   **Bay**
Bourke   Brewarrina   29   Collarenebri   Inverell   Glen Innes   **Grafton**   8   **135**
   Walgett   Narrabri   Mt Kaputar   Guyra   Woolgoolga
White   NP   *England*   **Coffs Harbour**

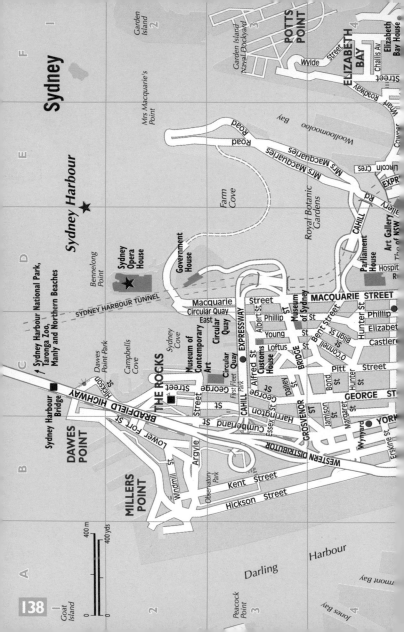

Sydney

Sydney Harbour

Goat Island

138

Darling Harbour

Peacock Point

Jones Bay

mont Bay

Hickson Street

Kent Street

Observatory Park

Windmill St

MILLERS POINT

Argyle St

Lower Fort St

BRADFIELD HIGHWAY

DAWES POINT

Sydney Harbour Bridge

↑ Sydney Harbour National Park, Taronga Zoo, Manly and Northern Beaches

SYDNEY HARBOUR TUNNEL

Dawes Point Park

Campbells Cove

THE ROCKS

George Street

Cumberland St

WESTERN DISTRIBUTOR

Harrington St

CAHILL EXPRESSWAY

Essex St

Grosvenor St

York St

Jamison St

Margaret St

Erskine St

Wynyard

YORK

GEORGE ST

Bond St

Hunter St

Pitt Street

Dalley St

George St

Alfred St

Customs House

Loftus St

Young St

Phillip St

Bridge St

Bent St

O'Connell St

Museum of Sydney

MACQUARIE STREET

Hunter St

Phillip St

Elizabeth

Castlere

Sydney Cove

Museum of Contemporary Art

Circular Quay

First Fleet Park

Circular Quay East

Macquarie Street

Bennelong Point

Sydney Opera House

Government House

Farm Cove

Royal Botanic Gardens

Mrs Macquarie's Point

Mrs Macquaries Road

Mrs Macquaries Road

Woolloomooloo Bay

Lincoln Cres

EXPR

Gallery Rd

CAHILL

Art Gallery of NSW

Parliament House

Hospit Rd

EXPR

ELIZABETH BAY

POTTS POINT

Wylde Street

Challis Av

Elizabeth Bay House

Wharf Roadway

Conve

Garden Island Naval Dockyard

Garden Island

400 m

400 yds

0

0

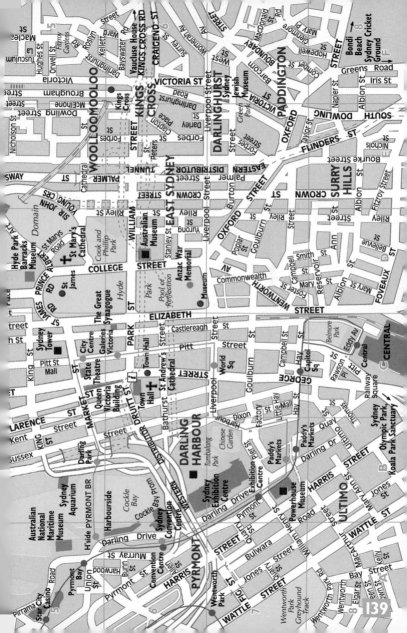

Bondi Beach 8
Sydney Cricket Ground

Macleay St
Maclee
St

5

Fitzroy St
Orwell St
Hughes St
Roslyn St
Kellett St
Bayswater Rd
Vaucluse House
KINGS CROSS RD
CRAIGEND ST

Ward
Av
Darlinghurst
Street
Roslyn
Gardens

Tusculum
La

Victoria
Street
Brougham
Street

McElhone
Street

Nicholson St

Dowling Street

WOOLLOOMOOLOO

Kings
Cross

KINGS
CROSS

VICTORIA ST

Forbes
St

Clapton
Place

Darley
St

Peters
St

Forbes

DARLINGHURST

West
St
Liverpool Street

Sydney
Jewish
Museum

Green
Park

Barcom
Av

Womerah Av

McDonald
Rd

Mary Pl
Glenmore Rd

Gurner
St

Hopewell St

Comber St

Greens Road

Napier St

Albion St
Iris St

PADDINGTON

OXFORD

SOUTH
DOWLING

FLINDERS ST

Nichols
St

Bourke Street

SWAY
ST

PALMER
ST

SIR JOHN
YOUNG CRS

Cathedral
St

St
TUNNEL
EASTERN

William
Street

Street
CROWN
STREET

Riley St

Burton
St

EAST
SYDNEY

Palmer
Street

Riley
Street

Yurong
St

OXFORD

Liverpool
St

DISTRIBUTOR

Poplar
St

Goulburn
St

Ann
St

Smith
St

Campbell
St

Mary
St

Albion
St

Bellevue
St

Riley
Street

Fitzroy Street

SURRY
HILLS

CROWN
ST

Street

FOVEAUX

Mary St

D

Hyde Park
Barracks
Museum

St Marys
Road

St Mary's
Cathedral

COLLEGE

Cook and
Phillip
Park

Australian
Museum

Stanley St

Anzac War
Memorial

Museum

Pool of
Reflection

AV

Commonwealth

Foster St

Reservoir St

WENTWORTH

STREET

PRINCE ALBERT RD

St
James

The Great
Synagogue

Hyde
Park

STREET

ST JAMES RD

treet

h St

t

Place

ELIZABETH

Street

Castlereagh

Street

Park
St

Sydney
Tower

City
Centre

Galeries
Victoria

Pitt

Street

World
Sq

Campbell St

Eddy Av

Belmore
Park

Rawson
Pl

PITT
St

Hay
St

Capitol
Sq

Central

C CENTRAL

LARENCE
ST

Kent
St

Sussex

King
St

Pitt St
Mall

State
Theatre

MARKET
ST

Queen
Victoria
Building

Town Hall

Town
Hall

St Andrew's
Cathedral

DRUITT ST

Bathurst

STREET

Liverpool

GEORGE

Dixon

Goulburn

Factory

St

Little Hay

Hay

Mall

St

Quay

Thomas St

Railway
Square

Sydney
Park,
Olympic Park,
Koala Park Sanctuary

B

Street

Street

CLARENCE

DARLING HARBOUR

Chinese
Garden

Tumbalong
Park

Sydney
Exhibition
Centre

Darling Drive

Paddy's
Markets

Exhibition
pier St

Pyrmont
St

Quay St

Darling Dr

HARRIS

ST

ULTIMO

Powerhouse
Museum

William Henry St

Quarry

WATTLE ST

Jones

Mary Ann St

MacArthur

Darling
Park

Sydney
Aquarium

Cockle
Bay

Sydney
PYRMONT BR

H'side

Harbourside

Cockle Bay prom

Convention
Centre

Darling   Drive

Sydney
Convention
Centre

DISTRIBUTOR

WESTERN

Bulwara

Bulwara

HARRIS

PYRMONT

STREET

Jones   Street

Wentworth
Park

William Henry St

Road

Australian
National
Maritime
Museum

Star City
Casino

Pirrama Rd

Pyrmont
Bay

Union St

Bunn St

Harwood St

Murray St

Convention
Centre

Pyrmont

HARRIS

Murray St

Wentworth

STREET

Quay St

WATTLE

ST

Wentworth
Park
Greyhound
Track

Wentworth Park

Jones
Bay

Elgar St

Kelly
St

Allen St

Edward St

Street

ULTIMO

5   6   7   8

139

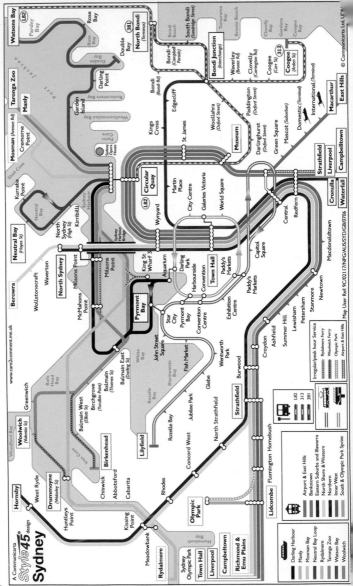

Sydney

140

Notes

Notes

Notes

Notes